WHAT DON'T KN[ow]

MEN, LOVE & SEX

COULD FILL A BOOK

New York Times best-selling author **David Zinczenko**,
editor of *Men's Health*, with **Ted Spiker**

RODALE

This edition first published in the UK in 2007 by
Rodale International Ltd
7–10 Chandos Street
London W1G 9AD
www.rodalebooks.co.uk

Printed and bound in the UK by CPI Bath using acid-free paper from sustainable sources.

1 3 5 7 9 8 6 4 2

A CIP record for this book is available from the British Library

ISBN-13: 978-1-4050-9988-2

This paperback edition distributed to the book trade by Pan Macmillan Ltd

Notice
Mention of specific companies, organizations or authorities in this book does not imply
endorsement by the publisher, nor does mention of specific companies, organizations or
authorities in the book imply that they endorse the book.
    Websites and telephone numbers given in this book were accurate at the time the book
went to press.

RODALE
LIVE YOUR WHOLE LIFE™

We inspire and enable people to improve their lives and the world around them

This book is dedicated to the thousands of men
who shared their innermost thoughts, feelings,
and desires with us. Here's to them, and to the thousands of women
who may come to love them even more because of it.

Contents

Contents

ACKNOWLEDGMENTS

MY DEEPEST THANKS to the extraordinarily talented, hard-working and dedicated people who have supported me, encouraged me, and inspired me. In particular:

Steve Murphy, whose courage and commitment to editorial quality have made Rodale the best publishing company in the world to work for.

The Rodale family, without whom none of this would be possible.

Ben Roter, whom I want to be when I grow up.

Ted and Liz Spiker, the world's best coauthor and his unerringly patient wife.

Stephen Perrine, the wisest consigliere any boss could ever have. Thanks for helping me live the best life.

Paige Nelson, the most admirable Nelson I've ever met.

Nicole Beland, whose wit and insight informed this book just as it has informed millions of *Men's Health* readers.

Fotoulla Euripidou and Emily McKeen, who designed the exclusive survey that pried open the thousands of tight-lipped men and women and got them to spill their guts.

Joe Heroun, a visual artist who has as much respect for words as he does for images.

The entire *Men's Health* editorial staff, the smartest and hardest-working group of writers, editors, researchers, designers, and photo directors in the industry.

A big shout-out to Liz Perl, Leigh Haber, Katrina Weidknecht, Kelly Schmidt, Sara Cox, Jennifer Giandomenico, Jackie Dornblaser, and everyone else who worked so hard and so fast to publish this book.

My brother, Eric, whose beautiful family is an inspiration to me.

My mother, Janice, who raised two of us nearly single-handedly. Your strength and kindness guide my every action.

My dad, Bohdan, who left this world way too early. I wish you were still here.

My uncle, Denny Stanz, the picture of youthfulness.

My stepmother, Mickey. Ditto.

And special thanks to: Dan Abrams, Jeff Anthony, Jeff Beacher, Matt Bean, Mary Ann Bekkedahl, Mark Bricklin, Michael Bruno, Marianne Butler, Adam Campbell, Monika Chiang, Jeff Csatari, Jack Essig, Jessica Guff, Jon Hammond and Karen Mazzotta, Erin Hobday, Samantha Irwin, George Karabotsos, Elaine Kaufman, Cindi Leive, Charlene Lutz, Mandy and Raina, Vincent Maggio, Matt Marion, Sandra Matthiessen, Paul McGinley, Peter Moore, Jeff Morgan, Sarah Peters, John Phelan, Bill Phillips, Richard and Sessa, Scott Quill, Amy Rosenblum, Eric Sacks, David Schipper, Robin Shallow, Larry Shire, Joyce Shirer, Rachel Sklar, Bill Stanton, Bill Stump, John Tayman, Pat and Steve Toomey, Marc Victor, and Kate White. Thanks for all the rock-solid advice and assistance. You guys rule.

What Women Don't Know About

Men, Love & Sex

Could Fill a Book

WHAT IS IT WITH MEN, ANYWAY?

Chances are you've spent more than your share of long nights on the phone, or hunched over coffee, or tossing back a margarita or two with your girlfriends, asking that very question.

And chances are, your girlfriends nodded and shrugged and sympathized, knowing exactly how you felt—that men are complex, confusing conundrums, riddles wrapped around enigmas and shrouded in beer and football stats.

Why don't men open up? Why do you sometimes feel that getting a guy to talk about his feelings requires a combination of hypnosis and psychic powers, along with maybe physical torture?

I'll admit, there's some truth to these stereotypes—sometimes we guys are better at expressing our feelings for the pizza delivery man than we are at expressing our feelings for you. And no doubt sometimes we do greet your postcoital nuzzlings with hearty snores. But the truth is, our goals and desires are a lot more aligned with yours than you might think. And the fact is that when a woman understands what a man truly wants—well, only then can she make him understand what she truly wants. And deep down, he wants more than anything to satisfy her.

In other words, all this ought to be a walk in the park. But somehow, we've turned that park into a minefield.

It's easy to fall back on the timeless "he-versus-she" arguments about the differences between men and women—what we want from each other, what we want out of love, what we want in relationships. But the problem isn't in what we want; it's in *how we communicate* what we want—and the fact that men and women do so in very different ways. The only way to get us to crack each other's codes is to delve deep into the psyches of both sexes—and that's exactly what this book does in a most unique and insightful way. You see, the truth is that men do share their feelings—their fears, their desires, even their deepest secrets. They've shared those feelings with me. And now I'm here to share their feelings with you.

A BREAKTHROUGH APPROACH TO UNDERSTANDING MEN

In our exclusive *Men, Love & Sex* poll, conducted by the polling firm Harris Interactive, we surveyed more than 5,000 men and women, asking them some intensely intimate questions—and eliciting some remarkably candid answers. And what our poll found was that men and women in fact have extraordinarily similar desires: We all want true love, a good sex life (that includes quickies as well as long, slow afternoons and everything in between), and relationships that last longer than the Easter weekend. What's different about us—and therefore what makes it so hard for us to find happiness together—is that we do a terrible job of communicating with one another. Between the smoke signals, silent treatments, and gender-specific Morse code, it's a wonder we ever get anything figured out, or get together at all.

All of us—men and women—spend a lot of time thinking about relationships. Sixty percent of men spend at least an hour a day thinking about their relationships or potential relationships (and you thought we were just daydreaming about sports), and 40 percent of women spend *more than two hours a day* thinking about their relationships. (Between the two of us, that's a combined 1,095 hours a year spent mulling over our love lives. Imagine if we dedicated that same time to, I don't know, trying to come up with an alternative to fossil fuel.) But despite all our time and efforts, two-thirds of people report that they experience relationship problems every two weeks.

So where's the breakdown? It's due in part to the fact that we're both too quick to buy into the stereotypes, which are in turn reinforced by our same-sex friends. Consider this: When women have a problem in their relationships, 82 percent—82 *percent!*—go to other women to talk about the problems. From where I stand, asking a woman to explain the feelings of a man is sort of like asking a politician to explain hip-hop music. We'd all be a lot better off if we looked for answers closer to the source.

Fortunately, you've come to the right place.

MEN SPEAK THEIR MINDS— AND HEARTS

In this survey, men talked. Boy, did they talk. They talked about love, insecurity, guys' nights out, what they secretly want from you in the bedroom, their biggest gripes with relationships, what you can do and say to make them happier. They confessed the little things that destroy relationships, and they revealed what they're scared of, what they're nervous about, and—most of all—they came clean with the truth about why they truly love and cherish you.

Ultimately, I have two goals here. Considering that more than 75 percent of women said they don't have men figured out, my first goal is to get you inside the minds of men so that you can better translate our verbal and nonverbal dictionaries. And that provides the foundation for my second goal: To give you the insights and actions that will strengthen and deepen your relationships.

For the last 12 years, I've worked at the largest men's magazine in the world. At *Men's Health*, we tackle relationship issues every month, we poll men about their secrets and their desires, and we research the newest studies about sex, love, and relationships. Every month, my job as the editor-in-chief is to give men what they want, and to do that, I have to understand what they want—not just when it comes to abs exercises and smoothie recipes, but also when it comes to women and relationships. I'm a professional student of men's hearts and minds, if you will.

But I also know that no matter how many years I've spent studying the male species, I can't possibly explain it as well as these guys can explain themselves. That's why, in this book, I'm going to give you unprecedented access to the real authorities on men, love, sex, and relationships: Men themselves—the thousands of them who answered our exclusive *Men, Love & Sex* poll, as well as hundreds of others who answered our questions via personal interviews and the *Men's Health* Web site. As you'll see throughout the book, these men were honest, sharp, and pointed about what they want—and open enough to share their fears and vulnerabilities in ways that just aren't acceptable in the course of typical relationships between men and women.

But this book is more than a dissection and inspection of male neurons; it's also a user's guide—a guide that will help you navigate through the sometimes-not-so-obvious actions, decisions, and thoughts that men have. And that is what will give you the knowledge and the power to make your own relationships better, stronger, sexier, and more satisfying.

Men can put on pretty good poker faces when it comes to revealing their feelings. But here, for the first time ever, we've got them to show their cards. Here are some of the hands you'll see . . .

MEN CONFESS ABOUT THEIR TRUE SELVES:
We're soft on the inside.

"Men are a lot like eggs. Under the right pressure, we can withstand any stress you put on us, but inside, we are soft and vulnerable. We are often so insecure that we can't confide in each other in the way women do, so we internalize quite a bit." —Michael, 30

We're much simpler than you think.
"Women express themselves in subtle ways that are open to interpretation, and you can never be sure if one interpretation is more accurate than the other. Men communicate more like a school textbook. When he says 1 + 1, he means 2, not 5, or 8, or 'I don't love you anymore.'" —Ryan, 31

We're more vulnerable to heartbreak than we let on.
"Men commit to women on an emotional level at an earlier age. Most men I know say they loved their first girlfriend. When she broke their heart, they decided not to go through the pain again." —Danny, 23

We're full of it because we want you to think we're strong.
"Most men are insecure and want someone to let them know they're worthwhile, no matter the amount of confidence they project." —Paul, 27

We're conflicted about our role in the relationship.
"Many men feel that they now have the dual responsibility of being the 1950s-style dad who supports the family and the 1990s-style sensitive guy." —Bryce, 29

MEN CONFESS ABOUT LOVE:
We're deeper than you might think.
"Most men want to fall in love. By that, I mean we want an emotional bond with a woman who is our friend, our supporter, and lover. We want to give love and share ourselves as best we can emotionally, physically, and spiritually." —Jeffrey, 28

We can be deeply in love; we just may show it in ways you don't always see.
"Love isn't all cuddly and sweetness. Women need to realize that for men, love is expressed a lot of times by what a man sacrifices for a woman—like sacrificing time at work or with friends. Most men like being in control, and power struggles are key to their daily lives, so giving up power voluntarily—choosing to do what she wants to do—is a very strong sign of love. Men just naturally aren't that selfless, unless they really care for a woman." —Bryan, 36

We may be most in love at the very times it doesn't seem like it.
"Love is comfortable, which can lead us to complacency. But just because we're not acting in love, it doesn't mean we're not." —Rick, 31

We want to keep it together when things are rough.
"The strongest and most appropriate expression of committed love is that when everything goes wrong, you do your best to put aside your own worries, frustrations, and fears, and try to help your partner as best you can, rather than freaking out and making matters worse. People will put up with a lot of crap if they know they can really count on someone's commitment in that way. It's the basis of a good relationship." —Jon, 29

We want it to happen naturally.
"Talking about love isn't going to make us love you any more."
—Bruce, 38

We fall in love much more easily than you think.
"It takes us longer to say the words, but we feel it sooner." —Simon, 28

We want you to take some of the pressure off us.
"Men prefer directness, assertiveness, and confidence. If a woman wants a man, she should be very open and honest about it. There's a scene in Conan the Destroyer where the young princess asks the female warrior how she should approach someone she likes, and the warrior replies, 'Grab him! Take him!'"
—Lucas, 35

MEN CONFESS ABOUT SEX:

We want foreplay as much as you do.
"Men are starved for affection for the most part — that includes cuddling, foreplay, caressing, soft touches. It's very important for a man's self-esteem and ego to have his partner tell him as well as show him through notes, cards, and initiating love-making." —Adam, 35

We truly want to please you.
"We're always scared we won't be good enough." —Robert, 34

We crave enthusiasm more than anything else.
"Show me that you really want me, that you're eager for me. That's the ultimate turn-on." —Joel, 40

We want sex to be like breaktime.
"We like when you get loud, and we don't like it when sex isn't as much fun for you as it is for us." —Andy, 40

We can be overwhelmed by sex.
"Women have no clue how powerful and overwhelming the male sex drive can be. They don't understand how it can consume us physically, mentally, and emotionally. Women only see the pleasure we get or seem to want. But that drive trumps the mind and has made all men that I know fools for very long moments."
—Len, 37

We're always assessing how you're doing.
"A woman climaxing is the most wonderful feeling to a man."
—Jeff, 30

Okay, so men are uncomplicated, vulnerable, and in need of love. Big deal—so are puppies. What else can I offer you, the reader?

Plenty. As part of our survey, we asked women to share with us their most pressing questions about male behavior, and how they can better know what men are thinking, feeling, and looking for. And I present many of those questions here, with answers that come straight from the hearts and minds of men themselves. In the pages that follow, you'll learn more about how men think, how they perceive you, and how most men are really 180 degrees away (give or take a few degrees) from the male stereotypes that are so often foisted upon us. Once you know that, you'll be able to bridge the communication gaps that divide men and women. You'll be able to strengthen the relationship you have now—or use your new insights to find the man who's perfect for you. And what you'll get in the end are better talks, better sex, better fighting, better understanding, better love, better relationships, and a better life. Not just for you, but for us guys too.

Above all, what should get through to you over the course of these pages is this:

We dig you.

We want you.

We want it to work with you.

And, really, all we want in return is for you to think the same exact thing.

Chapter 1

What Makes a Man Fall in Love?

Why we can't let love in until you've shown us the way — and the simple words that can unleash our deepest affections.

QUESTION: Guys, do you believe you've met your soul mate?

Yes, I'm with her right now: . . . . 53 PERCENT

Yes, but we're no longer together: . . . . 14 PERCENT

Yes, but we were never together as a couple: . . . 9 PERCENT

No: . . . . 24 PERCENT

THINK OF A GREAT RELATIONSHIP AS though it were a great meal: A delicious steak of sexual passion accompanied by a fine wine of romance and commitment. Both of us want it all — the perfect, satisfying meal. And we need both parts of the meal — steak by itself is dry and unsatisfying; and wine will get you tipsy, but it won't satisfy your hunger. Now, before the metaphor police revoke my license, let me push this analogy further: Men are a little more focused on the meat of the relationship, and women a bit more on the wine. But both sexes want to get up from the table completely satisfied.

Need evidence? More than three-quarters of men believe in soul mates. And when we asked our guys to choose between meeting the love of their life or having amazing sex for six months, 92 percent chose falling in love. (The other 8 percent were probably Maxim readers.) Consider what these three men said about the experience of falling in love:

- ►*"We need to feel love, loyalty, and chemistry above all else,"* says Ian, 31.

- ►*"Men also feel the butterflies and giddiness that women do when they're in love,"* says Robert, 26.

- ►*"Women don't realize most guys are in love long before they are willing to admit it to anyone,"* says Drew, 30.

So why then does it always seem like women are leading the relationship toward commitment, and men need to be dragged along like a toddler to a dentist appointment? Because in the early-on Stratego game of dating, we need to see where you're moving first. Consider this: Less than half of men say they're typically the first ones to say "I love you" in a relationship, and more women than men initially broach the subject of taking the relationship to the next level.

That points to the notion that what men really want when it comes to love is your assurance—your permission, really— that it's okay to let the butterflies out of the cage.

Michael, a 37-year-old restaurant owner, says he's cautious about expressing himself early on—not because he's complacent or wants to play games or wants to make the woman squirm like a mouse in a cat's mouth. He holds back because he's waiting to get the signal that it's okay to press the accelerator.

SAY THIS, NOT THAT!

SAY THIS: *University was a breeze, but I was terrible at drinking games.*

NOT: *I graduated with first-class honors.*

BECAUSE: *Perfection is intimidating. Flaws are lovable.*

SAY THIS: *What makes you happy?*

NOT: *Where do you see yourself in five years?*

BECAUSE: *He needs to know you're interested in him, not a lifestyle.*

SAY THIS: *I love my family—even if they're hard to deal with.*

NOT: *I can't deal with my family.*

BECAUSE: *The more accepting you are of them, the more accepting you'll be of him.*

"I love to hear that I'm her dream come true, or some version of that, if that's the case," he says. "I need a little praise and attention, just as much as she needs it from me. That's the sign I need. Then, I know I can give her what she needs."

Chris, 29, a recently married public defender, agrees. "Men need to be told that they're wanted," he says. "Women forget that if they like a nice guy, that the nice guy might be too nervous to tell them what he feels." And then he added this interesting insight: "Women need to be more open to being hurt the way guys are every day."

Hold on a second. Guys are hurt more often than women?

Hmm. Think about it. In the romance game, it's usually the man who makes the first move (usually after you've dropped him countless hints waiting for him to finally pick up on them). But in doing so, men open themselves up to more rejection than a telemarketing trainee. And believe me, even George Clooney has a psychic master list of turn-downs that he still winces over from time to time.

So once a man has crossed that first barrier—okay, you like him, it's safe—he's reluctant to cross the next. Like monkeys in a lab, we've been shocked plenty of times before, and if we're in a safe place with you, we're happy simply to stay there. So it's a delicate balance—a woman needs to signal that it's okay for him to take the next step, without making him feel as if he's being pushed toward it. Let him know that you feel there's something really special between you. Let him know it's okay if he lets himself feel that, too. But proceed cautiously—there's danger ahead, as you'll see.

HOW DO I KNOW WHERE THIS RELATIONSHIP IS HEADING?

I've been seeing a guy for about three weeks, and I feel like it's going to be pretty serious. After the first two dates, we've been seeing each other a lot. Last week, we got together twice during the week and twice on the weekend. I'd like to talk about where this is headed, but I don't want to scare him away. I just want to make sure we're both on the same page about where we are, whether we're seeing other people, and where this might go. What's he thinking?

WHAT IT MEANS WHEN

. . . He says he'll call and doesn't

He's thinking like a jockey at the start of a horse race. He doesn't want to pull out of the gates too fast. Waiting a few days allows him to set a comfortable pace before he makes a move. Any longer than that probably means he's pulled himself up and plans on entering another race, another day.

. . . He calls you right away

While he knows he risks you thinking that he's more desperate than a virginal octogenarian, he's trying to establish in your mind that he's not a game-player, whether he ends up being one or not.

. . . He e-mails instead of calls after a first date

He's written 14 drafts of that e-mail to convey the perfect balance of witty, flirty, and complimentary without making it seem like he tried too hard to be witty, flirty, and complimentary. He doesn't fear conversation; he's just banking on the fact that his first e-mail popping into your inbox gives you as much of a jolt as you give him.

He's thinking that, three weeks into dating, he doesn't want to have this conversation. To him, that's a relationship birth announcement. *Today, we welcome the birth of a beautiful committed couple, weighing in at eight dates, two movies, and six orgasms (five for him, one for her): It's Tom and Sarah! Congratulations!* It's too formal, too official, too planned. And that formality serves as the fire extinguisher to the initial spark he's been feeling. "The only thing worse than a woman who doesn't show any interest after a few dates is a woman who shows too much," says Anthony, 25. Terry, 32, adds: "Slow down. Please don't tell us that you love us after three weeks." Think of it this way. You know how you don't like when he skips the foreplay and goes right to the sex? When you talk about the status of a relationship too early, it's like skipping the foreplay of pursuit and going right to the private parts of commitment. If he's seeing you four times a week, then it's a good sign that your relationship is headed in the right direction. Just let him have some fun—and some mystery—while he's getting there.

HOW DO I KNOW WHEN IT'S TIME TO TELL HIM MY FEELINGS?

I've been seeing a man for only two months. Perfect guy. He's funny, has a great job, I love hanging out with him. We even took this great weekend vacation together and everything seemed to click. I just have this feeling that this is going to work, and I'm pretty sure he feels the same way. I don't want to blow it, and while I obviously don't want to pretend to be somebody that I'm not, I also don't want to do anything that could jeopardize the relationship. Any hints for how to take things from here?

Two months may seem like a blip on the relationship radar for many people, but for some guys, that qualifies as a full-fledged era. At this point, men certainly want some honesty. "If she is more open with me, I'll be more open with her, especially at the beginning when you're both feeling each other out, emotionally," says Warren, 33. But that comes with a caution. Feel free to be honest about your feelings and let him know what you're thinking, but don't make assumptions about his. Don't use the word *us.* At this stage, you'll solidify your primo status if you talk about what you like about *him,* what you get out of a relationship with *him,* what turns you on about *him. Us* scares him; *him* excites him. (Yes, we're our own favorite subject, but that's just human nature—many women are the same.) It's a way of saying you love the relationship and want it to go further while giving him the ego-boosting rush he craves—all without making him think you're brushing up on the four Cs of diamond shopping. At this still-early stage, that's a secret to tip-toeing between giving him permission to love and giving him a reason to leave.

Male Mysteries

23

Percentage of men who say "I love you" to escape from arguments

SHOULD I GIVE HIM AN ULTIMATUM?

My live-in boyfriend and I have been seeing each other for about a year and a half, and we've been living together for somewhere around six months. I'm 31 and my family is giving me a hard time—like I should just go ahead and move on if he's not going to be the one because I'm wasting time. My best friend even says to me that there's no way he's going to marry me now that we're living together because he's getting all the sex of a nonmarried relationship without the commitment. I've debated a lot about giving him an ultimatum or a deadline, but something tells me that's a bad idea—and I'm not sure what I'd do if his answer wasn't the one I wanted to hear. How will I know if he's ever going to be ready to make the next step?

You may think that men are afraid of the marriage commitment because we want to leave options open, because we're waiting for something better, or because we fear it'll be the official end of hot-tub sex. Jay, 30, says a man's hesitation isn't about indifference; it's actually the opposite. "Men are just as unsure about the relationship thing as women," he says.

WONDERING WOMAN

My husband is always telling me that his friends think I'm hot. Why does he get such pleasure out of that?

Good job, good car, good bank account, good body, good wife—together, they help make up the equation that forms the hierarchy of alpha males. Plus, you're hot.

"I'm getting married in a couple months to a woman I love deeply, who I know will be a fantastic wife and mother to my future children. Is she my soul mate? Tough question, but if not, she's pretty darn close." When we decide we want to be married, we want to do the right thing—for both of us. So should you give him an ultimatum? I don't think so. If you've been honest with him about your feelings for him—for him, not for "the relationship"—then you're probably at the point in your relationship where you should be able to ask him straight up about his feelings for you, and his feelings about marriage. If he can't tell you what he thinks and what he feels, well, that's probably your answer.

> **Male Mysteries**
>
> # 26
>
> Percentage of men who think that a quiet night at home is the date that puts them most in the mood *(MH)*

MASCULINITY MASTERED: What You Now Know About Men

• If you want to talk about the long-term possibilities of your relationship, there's such a thing as premature enunciation. Don't be too clear, too early, about what you think you want from the relationship.

• We're not scared of falling in love; we're scared of being told that we're falling in love. Focus on your feelings for him, not your feelings for the relationship.

• A man is more willing to make a move that shows his feelings if you do it first. If not, he'll probably wait for a very long time before finally getting the confidence to let you know how he feels.

SAY THIS TONIGHT!

The sexiest thing a woman ever said to Joe, 36:
"Damn."

The sexiest thing Amy, 23, ever said to a man:
"Baby, I want you right now."

Chapter 2

Why Do Guys Always Need to Be in Charge?

How you can deepen your relationship by
knowing when and how to take the lead.

QUESTION: Guys, how would you rate your current sex life?

It's an A: . . . . 16 PERCENT

It's a B: . . . . 28 PERCENT

It's a C: . . . . 24 PERCENT

It's a D: . . . . 14 PERCENT

It's an F: . . . . 18 PERCENT

F YOU'RE SHOCKED BY THE ABOVE STATISTICS,
well, I'm not surprised. Aren't all guys just happy to get
some? Isn't sex to a man like leftovers to a dog—we don't care
if it's a ready meal or filet mignon? Clearly, that assumption
is wrong. Fifty-six percent of the men we polled rated their
sex lives as no better than a C. Out of 2,500 men, that's 1,400 who find
their bedroom action unsatisfying—and surely all of them can't be dating
Dame Edna.

What's going on here?

The men I've spoken with—through the *Men, Love & Sex* poll, through my work at *Men's Health*, and in my thirty-something years of listening to other guys—all seem to have one desire: They all wish their girlfriends or wives would take the lead in the bedroom once in a while.

On a scale of 1 to 10 (with a 1 being an anesthetized surgical patient and a 10 being a coked-up rocker), men rate the sexual aggressiveness of their current or most recent wife or girlfriend as a 5. What do we want? According to our poll, it's an 8. Add in the fact that when men rate their best sexual experience—as in, best sexual experience *ever*—one common theme stands out: *She* takes charge. Take these guys as examples:

► Andy, 31, a Web designer, says the best sex he ever had was when his girlfriend at the time steered the entire sexual situation—even though it involved her much more than it involved him. *"She spontaneously masturbated in front of me, and she didn't let me touch her or get myself undressed,"* Andy says. *"She asked me to tell her that she was turning me on (and she was!), so as I told her how sexy she was, she came closer and closer until she finally did shudder to an orgasm."*

► John, a 27-year-old law student, says that he's turned on by the fact that his girlfriend's aggressiveness in bed is a little bit like a man's. *"Recently I came home and she was dressed like the innocent school girl. Skirt, glasses, stockings—the whole look,"* he says. *"She took control of me and rode me over and over until she had an orgasm. God, do I love it. The sex is so great."*

► Kyle, 36, who's been married for four years, says that aggressiveness isn't necessarily about being kinky or crazy or doing anything that the woman's uncomfortable with. He says, *"One time, my wife seduced me first by phone, while I was at work, just by telling me that she couldn't wait for me to get home. Then when I walked in, she had left me a note at the front table to 'get comfortable and come to bed,' where she was waiting. Then we had some awesome sex."*

SAY THIS, NOT THAT!

SAY THIS: *I really want this relationship to work.*

NOT: *I don't know where this relationship is going.*

BECAUSE: *Neither does he.*

SAY THIS: *I would love to meet your parents.*

NOT: *Why aren't you inviting me home for Christmas?*

BECAUSE: *He won't know it means a lot to you until you tell him.*

SAY THIS: *I want to live with you, but I'm willing to wait.*

NOT: *We should be living together by now.*

BECAUSE: *Men move faster when they're not under pressure.*

► Joseph, 31, who's been married for five years, says his best time came when his wife took the lead throughout the whole session. *"I came home from work and the lights were low and music was playing and my wife was dressed in lingerie,"* he says. *"She met me at the door and we kissed and touched each other all over and then she pulled me on top of her and grabbed my butt and tried to pull me in deep as she groaned, and then we both had an orgasm and fell asleep."*

But you're probably thinking: Don't men like to take the lead? Doesn't it excite a man to feel like he's in control? To which I would respond: Brad and Angelina. If they're the universally accepted sexiest couple in the world, then I ask you: Who do you think gives the orders in bed in that relationship?

Exactly.

Men like to think of themselves as the hunters. But we don't necessarily want to be hunting possum, and we sure don't want you to roll over and play dead; we'd rather feel like the hunt was between two creatures of equal sexual power, and that once we have you in our sights, you'll be just as aggressive as we are. We want you to "meet our urgency," as Bruce Springsteen might have put it. You have the ability to recharge us, sexually—in the form of assertiveness, seduction, and, dare I say it, even a little nagging. *Touch me here. Clothes off. Get on top of me. Again. Now.*

That's the kind of ordering around no man will ever get tired of hearing.

HOW FREE SHOULD I BE DURING THE FIRST TIME WITH A NEW GUY?

I've been seeing a guy for a few weeks, and we've messed around a fair amount but haven't actually slept together. I know I shouldn't really be comparing myself to other women he's slept with, but of course, there's a side of me that wants to be his best, that wants him to really remember it. On the other hand, I don't want him to think I'm a whip-using weirdo. What's enough to impress a guy in bed without him thinking you're too crazy or maybe even worse, too experienced?

You're right: There's a difference between showing enthusiasm and putting on a production worthy of a Broadway show. Your goal should be to show

WHAT IT MEANS WHEN

. . . He doesn't sleep over

Men are practical— he's not thinking about the symbolic nature of leaving your apartment after orgasm. If he has work the next morning, he wants to wake up with easy access to his own wardrobe and his own razor.

. . . He does sleep over

Men are practical— he's not thinking about the symbolic nature of falling asleep after having sex. If he doesn't have work the next morning, it's easier to stay than to pick up and go.

. . . He has freshly grown facial hair somewhere below the bottom lip

He's recently been through a bad breakup.

him that you're sensual, open-minded, and, most of all, that you're into him. What you don't need is to prove to us that you're part cowgirl, part trapeze artist, and part opera singer. The thrill of the first time—the proof that a woman like you wants a poor schlub like us—is enough to make it special.

For example, Marcus, 29, a landscape designer, says that the first time he has sex with a woman isn't the true indicator of how their sexual relationship is going to be. "I've been with women who are usually pretty conservative the first time," he says. "But after that, you usually get a better sense of what they're like sexually. The thing that really turns me on with a new woman is pretty simple. It's when she shows that she's just hungry for me, like if she doesn't have me now, she'll go crazy." For most men a great sexual experience is just like a great road trip—we want a partner who's enthusiastic, adventurous, who smells good, and who knows how to drive a stick.

We don't need a stunt driver.

HOW DO MEN RATE A WOMAN IN BED?

Look, I know how it is. A man is never going to criticize a woman in bed, or tell her that she's anything but great—because if he does, he knows he'll never get any ever again. But how does a woman know if a guy thinks she's really good in bed?

I once worked for a boss who demoted an employee not by calling him into his office and giving him the news straight-up, but by posting an org chart on the office bulletin board showing the poor guy a level lower than where he thought he was. Not the best way to build employee loyalty, but it illustrates a point: Nobody likes to give bad news. And more important, nobody likes to give bad news to someone they have to be with day in and day out.

What men say when they're out of the line of fire, however, is that they're not looking at your "performance," or comparing you to other lovers. They're looking at your enthusiasm—how you respond to their touch, how much you seem to want to touch them. "I've had great lovers. One ex-girlfriend tried to do everything different every time—red scarves over the lights, new positions, you name it, and it was great," says Brad, a 32-year-old sporting goods rep. "But I'm with someone else. The sex is totally different with her and more traditional, but it's still great and fun and intense, just a different kind of great." In a guy's mind, we're more concerned about the next time we're going to have sex—not the last time. Men are to sex what Wile E. Coyote was to the Roadrunner—even if we feel like we got an anvil dropped on our head, we're already plotting our next approach.

Male Mysteries

72

Percentage of men who initiate sex more than half the time *(MH)*

But if you really want to know what he thinks of you in bed, here's the sign: You know how some men can be on their best relationship behavior when they're pursuing sex—by being extra loving, romantic, and caring? A man who has just had great sex will also be on his best relationship behavior afterward.

HOW MUCH SEX DO MEN NEED?

I've been married for six years, and the amount of sex my husband and I have dropped off pretty significantly—from three or four times a week to maybe once every two weeks. I can't really give you a great reason why—probably a combination of being tired, and maybe feeling like it's become too much of a routine. But I sometimes worry that it's not enough for my husband—I want him to be satisfied, but it's hard to find the time and energy to make it happen more often. Do you think our relationship is in trouble?

Here's the thing—most men understand, and accept, the realities of growing into adulthood. (I know, this doesn't explain guys who act like Charlie Sheen, but that one's got me flummoxed.)

WONDERING WOMAN

I casually mention that he needs a haircut (because it's so long and stringy he looks homeless) and he seems to purposely wait another three weeks before going to the barber. What's up with that?

Because 20 years ago, his parents told him when to get a haircut, where to get a haircut, and how to get a haircut. He likes being told he can't take care of himself about as much as you'd like being told that you're running behind on waxing appointments. He has a mirror. He'll go when he has a chance.

The fact is, we too feel the pressures of jobs, kids, even body issues, and we too wonder if we're giving you the sex you need. The rapid-fire sexual machines that we were when we first met may become more like popguns, and the wild inventiveness we once brought to lovemaking can turn into something more akin to assembly line work. John, who's 43 and has been married for 15 years, says that he's a realist. "Do I expect to have sex with my wife three times a week, the way we did when we first got married? No. Even I don't have the energy for that, as much as I may think I want to," he says.

And again, most of us are fine with that. (Shut up, Charlie Sheen!) But as with anything, a drop in quantity shouldn't be accompanied by a simultaneous drop in quality. John continues: "There are times when I can tell my wife is having sex with me because she feels it's her 'duty' since it's been a while since the last time we had sex. Nothing's worse than that feeling." The key is not to worry about frequency, but to set aside time when both of you can be equally into your lovemaking and make a point of savoring the experience. After all, the older we get, the more we understand why a single bottle of fine Scotch is worth more than five cases of cheap bourbon.

MASCULINITY MASTERED: What You Now Know About Men

• Sometimes, the thing that makes sex most memorable is that it begins with you wanting it.

• When it comes to your involvement in sex, noise always trumps toys.

• As a relationship matures, a man will stay satisfied if the emphasis is on quality, not quantity.

SAY THIS TONIGHT!

The sexiest thing a woman ever said to Craig, 28.
"I love your body."

The sexiest thing Diane, 31, ever said to a man:
"I can't get enough of you, your skin, your touch, your eyes."

Chapter 3

Why Does Our Sex Life Run Hot and Cold?

Our lovemaking begins the moment we open our eyes in the morning. Once you're attuned to his simple love signs, you'll know how to maximize the romance — in and out of bed.

QUESTION: Guys, what's the most important thing in a relationship?

Friendship: .... 62 PERCENT

Similar life goals and dreams: .... 31 PERCENT

Sex: .... 8 PERCENT

STRAIGHT UP. SOME MEN WANT nothing more from a relationship than 20 minutes of wake-the-whole-street sex (okay, it's more like 3½ minutes, but who's counting?), and some of us will go through all the lovey-dovey motions it takes to get it. But those guys are about as representative of men as Paris Hilton is of women. Yes, some of us *are* as shallow as a reflecting pool. But most of us are thinking bigger—and more romantic—thoughts.

There are certainly times when men are looking for nothing more than a fast woman and a faster getaway car. But the men in our survey made two things very clear: Yes, they love sex. And no, it's not how they define the success of a relationship. In fact, 63 percent of men say that a woman who sleeps with them on the first date probably won't be the woman they marry, and more than half of men say that sex without an emotional relationship isn't even possible for them. What's more revealing is that men are even a little put out that they're stereotyped as heavy-breathing, penis-swinging heathens whose lives revolve around finding the next territory to explore. To many men, sex only represents one (very sweet) slice of the relationship pie.

► *"Women need to understand our need for affection,"* says Keith, 26, a radio-show producer. *"It's about acceptance, reward, relief, and love as much as anything else. It's just that we need [physical affection] up front to feel loved and wanted."*

► *"We are no different than women in what we want. We are looking for that one person who will make us and keep us happy for the long run,"* says Bob, 33, an IT manager. *"We're looking for women who will be the same person while they're married as they are when they're dating."*

► *"I think that women mostly don't understand that relationships can be—and often are—just as emotionally binding for men as they are for women,"* says Todd, 27.

► *"We think about sex a whole lot, but we care more about women than we care about sex,"* says Reed, 37.

► *"I love a woman who is very sensual. A woman unafraid of telling me what she's thinking is the girl for me,"* says Jerry, 32.

Now, take a look at the story of Richard, who's a 31-year-old architect. When he was in his twenties, he had been seeing a woman for a little less than a year. They had what he says was the most unbelievable sex of his life.

SAY THIS, NOT THAT!

SAY THIS: *I'm so hot. I can't wait to have sex with you again.*

NOT: *We haven't done it in weeks!*

BECAUSE: *Stating the obvious won't make it happen.*

SAY THIS: *Let's go to that dark little bistro this weekend and make out at the table.*

NOT: *We don't do anything romantic anymore.*

BECAUSE: *Give him a plan, and he'll run with it.*

SAY THIS: *Untie my bustier with your teeth!*

NOT: *Do you want me to wear lingerie?*

BECAUSE: *The answer is no—until he sees you in it.*

"I mean, incredible," he says. "There's nothing this woman wouldn't do. It was like every time we had sex, she'd try to one-up herself. Then some nights, she'd just lean over, and ask me what I wanted—like she was some kind of waitress and I could order up anything from her menu. If I was really tired, I could just say that I wanted oral, and bingo, that's what I got."

Male Mysteries

34

Percentage of men who say their best sexual experience was based on the way their partner looked naked

Richard says it was a good relationship, but they had more problems than a decade-old hard drive. For one, he felt that they were at different places in their careers and lives. Besides partying with friends, they disagreed on how to spend weekends (he enjoyed being outside, she didn't). And, deep down, he never really trusted her, because he once suspected that she strayed, though he never had proof. "One night, when she mentioned something about how she liked my parents so much that they'd make great in-laws, it hit me that I didn't see myself having a family with her," he says. "We ended up breaking up a few weeks later. The sex was unbelievable, but it was hardly worth staying in the relationship."

Maybe it took Richard too much time to realize it, and maybe his amazing sex life clouded him into thinking that his long-term relationship would ultimately work. Of course, there's a part of most men that wants tabloid-worthy sexual escapades, but the reality is that men—even though we love, crave, and sometimes can't get enough sex—aren't as superficial as a paper cut. We're a lot deeper than you think.

DO GUYS USE ROMANCE TO GET SEXUAL FAVORS?

A couple weeks ago, my boyfriend said he wanted to plan this big, special night for us. No reason, just that he felt like going out and doing something fun. So he did—he went all out. Nice restaurant, then a fun little show at a small theater, then he took me dancing (which he never does). He even gave me a card and wrote why he loves me. I, of course, was especially turned on so we had some pretty high-quality sex that night. But as soon as he finished, he kinda flopped over and fell asleep. And then the next day it was back to our normal routine. I know the lengths guys go to for sex, but as nice as the night was, it was almost as if it was one big get-me-horny sham. Am I reading that right?

WHAT IT MEANS WHEN

. . . He cuddles after sex

It was unbelievable. Thank you.

. . . He rolls over to go to sleep after sex

It was unbelievable. Thank you.

. . . He says "I love you" for the first time (during sex)

It was unbelievable. Thank you.

Well, not exactly. Think of guys as machines with two separate gas tanks. One's the sexual, physiological one. And you know how that one works: we can use it once and then we (at least those of us who aren't Colin Farrell) have to wait a little while before we can go to the reserves to use it again. In a lot of ways, we have a romantic gas tank that works the same way. We can use it, but it takes a little while before we have the energy to use it again.

See, men want to be romantic heroes—and we'd happily be your Romeos even if we knew it wouldn't result in sex. Just like the famous rock band that jams itself into a tiny club for a gig, we love the tangible rewards of what we do, but we also enjoy doing it just for kicks. It's the satisfaction of pulling off a sensational romantic performance that turns us on.

That said, we don't always have the time, energy, or creativity to sweep you off your feet time and again. "It's not that I don't want to be romantic all the time," says Jay, 33, a pharmaceutical sales rep who's been in a relationship for a year. "But sometimes it feels like it takes a lot of energy to pull off the kind of romance she wants." Kenny, 24, adds: "I'm romantic and sappy. It's just hard to show sometimes." There are times when we do have the time, energy, and wherewithal to blow your mind with our expressions of love, just as there are times when you blow our minds with your expressions of sexual passion. But one doesn't depend on the other. Sometimes he just wants to be romantic. Just like sometimes you just want some sex.

WILL GIVING A GUY SEX GET ME THE AFFECTION I WANT?

I don't get it. I know—especially after talking to my friends—that I'm about as sexually aggressive as it gets. I wear sexy clothes, try new things, love having sex, and can treat a man's

body right. But here's the deal: Over the past two years, I haven't had a relationship last more than four or five months. I like to think I'm also smart and funny and fun to be around, so I don't know what's going on. Any thoughts?

You hear the word 'connection' a lot in TV dating shows. But that word resonates because it has meaning to both men and women: The truth is that a man defines connection not only by the sparks that fly when lips connect, but also the sparks that fly when words come out of them. "Men aren't only absorbed in sex," says Matthew, 31, a physician's assistant. "Anyone can have sex with me. We, or I, want a woman with brains, a sense of humor, talents, responsibility, and maturity—more or less the same traits that they look for in a guy." I can't speak for what happened with you and your previous boyfriends, but I can tell you that good sex makes good relationships great. The only thing that good sex does to bad relationships is make them last a little longer than they probably should.

Male
Mysteries

32

Percentage of men who say they've stayed in a relationship because of the great sex

WHY DO GUYS BED US AND BOLT?

The last guy I dated did everything right. He took me out, complimented me without coming off like a used-car salesman, called when he said he would, and we had great conversations. After three dates, we had sex, but then it was all downhill. We went out again, but he said it didn't "feel right." I know all guys aren't like that—because I'm dating a great one right now—but still, I hate feeling like guys are only after some pillow time. How do I know if a man is interested in me—or just in getting me into bed?

There's clearly a segment of men who play the role of sexual comic-book villain. By day, he's disguised as a romantic, loving, chivalrous man who will do anything for you; by night, he slips out of his street clothes and into the guise of his alter-ego, The Diddler. And when he puts his clothes back on, presto, he's gone.

But you know what? That guy's the aberration—the one who's giving the rest of us a bad name. Most men truly want relationships to work out. "I'm 33, and I've dated a lot of women," says Dwayne, a book editor. "If I'm not seeing someone, I go on at least one or two dates every week, and I can honestly say

WONDERING WOMAN

I would love to hang by my ankles from the ceiling during sex, so why doesn't he seem to crave funky new positions?

Perhaps in his previous sex life, he was relegated to being Missionary Man. After being denied sexual variety for a long time, he's likely forgotten about (or hesitant to ask about) the sweet taste of upside-down orgasms. Want to increase the craving? Then help him out by initiating the temptations.

that I go into most of the dates—not all of them—with the thought, or maybe it's hope, that it'll work into something more than just a couple of glasses of wine and a plate of pasta." While it may be difficult to know a potential date's real intentions, I think you can find out a lot about him by exploring the women he used to date. Sometimes, you can use his past relationships to find out his intentions for the future. If he's coming right out of a long relationship, it's a sign that he's likely more interested in one-time action than meaningful interaction.

MASCULINITY MASTERED:
What You Now Know About Men

• Great sex, over the long term, doesn't mean much if the rest of the relationship is mediocre.

• We're as in tune to how you treat us out of bed as we are in tune to how you treat us in it.

• Sex shouldn't be used as a relationship seatbelt. You can keep him trapped in a relationship by using your body, but if he's not satisfied with your mind, your personality, and everything else, he will eventually find a way to unbuckle.

SAY THIS TONIGHT!

The sexiest thing a woman ever said to James, 24:

"I love you so much, but if you're not naked within 10 seconds, my clothes are going back on."

The sexiest thing Maria, 32, ever said to a man:

"C'mere."

THE BEST SEX HE EVER HAD

"It was in a hotel. We would have sex, then we would sleep, then when one of us woke up, we'd pleasure the sleeping person. In eight hours, we had sex eight times—the last time for 50 minutes." —Shane, 21

"The best sex was after my partner and I got back together after an eight-month breakup because it was like being with a new partner but knowing exactly what pleased her." —Lyle, 29

"The best was when we went out for the night all dressed up, and she kept teasing me the whole night. When we finally got home, it was like we were 16." —Danny, 28

"She tore my clothes off, she was so eager. We had sex for 20 minutes and then fell asleep in each other's arms." —Ken, 24

"She came home from work wearing a black skirt, thigh highs, and a tight white blouse. She looked at me with a devilish look and said she wasn't wearing any panties. We had sex right there on the floor." —Tony, 26

"We climaxed at the same time." —Michael, 25

"Our best is when we talk about our fantasies while we're having sex." —Tyler, 23

"In a car on the top level of a department store parking garage. During a thunderstorm." —Wayne, 38

"It was totally out of the blue. I walked in the house and she was hot and ready. She took me apart in the kitchen." —Ivan, 34

"We dressed up in Halloween costumes." —Brendan, 33

Chapter 4

Why Don't Men Talk Like Women Do?

The real truth about why men hold back, and how you can draw a man out using three simple tactics.

QUESTION: Guys, how would you grade your happiness level in your current relationship?

It's an A: .... 37 PERCENT

It's a B: .... 38 PERCENT

It's a C: .... 18 PERCENT

It's a D: .... 5 PERCENT

It's an F: .... 2 PERCENT

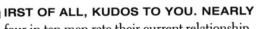

IRST OF ALL, **KUDOS TO YOU. NEARLY** four in ten men rate their current relationship an A. And 98 percent give their love lives a passing grade. The reason? Because you're pretty darn amazing.

And there's the great irony: Men, in general, are pretty happy in their relationships. And yet women—the very people responsible for making guys so happy—spend a great deal of time fretting over whether their men want to stay in the relationship or are waiting to catch the next bus out of it. Indeed, women spend so much time fretting that they often ask men to talk more about . . . gasp! . . . their feelings. And the one thing that can make a contented guy discontented is being asked to talk about his feelings. It's like cooking up a great soufflé, and then opening the oven to check on it—and presto, the soufflé goes flat.

It's not that you should never ask a man about his feelings. But it's all about technique: you need to coax him to that place where he can share; pushing him just makes him stubborn.

► *"We have feelings too that need to come out, but we need help in getting them out,"* says Grant, 35.

► *"Men may not always want to talk about their feelings, but that doesn't mean that they aren't invested in the relationship,"* says Stan, 31.

► *"We're taught to keep most things to ourselves so we don't appear as weak or unable to make quick or firm decisions,"* says Billy, 27.

► *"You want us to talk? Then please don't ask us our feelings,"* says Colin, 24.

► *"Women don't know that most men want an emotional connection, but in general, we have trouble communicating, and we just internalize what we're feeling more. I know I'm better writing my feelings than talking about them,"* says Garry, 29.

The problem for a lot of guys is that talking feelings with a woman is like talking French with a native Parisian. No matter how hard we study, we'll never master the language with quite the same fluency. So you—the hot French lady in this equation—need to make things a little simpler for us.

SAY THIS, NOT THAT!

SAY THIS: *What do you think about that?*

NOT: *How do you feel about that?*

BECAUSE: *He knows how to answer the first question, but the second one makes him nervous.*

SAY THIS: *I wish I could say this in a way that makes more sense to you.*

NOT: *You don't understand me.*

BECAUSE: *Miscommunication is a two-way street.*

SAY THIS: *Let's go for a drive.*

NOT: *Let's sit down and talk.*

BECAUSE: *Men are less tense when they're doing something physical.*

SAY ANYTHING: *Once*

NOT: *Ten times*

BECAUSE: *To a guy, repetition makes a statement meaningless.*

From our end, there are two things we'd prefer you didn't do. One, don't directly ask about the f-word—feelings. Say the word feelings to a man and it's like clipping your toenails during a striptease—total turn-off. The reason? We have feelings, but we don't have the access to them that you do. So every conversation that's pointedly about our feelings seems to us like the last 15 minutes of a TV police drama, where we're the accused and you're the clever detective, poking a finger in our face and hinting that you know just a little more than we do.

And you do know a little more than we do. You know how you feel. And we don't know how we feel. So if you want us to talk, then help us speak your language—by speaking a little of ours.

Male Mysteries

27

Percentage of men who say they primarily fight with their wives or girlfriends about the fact that they don't share or talk about their feelings

"One night, my wife got mad at me for something really stupid—the fact that I had plans to go to lunch with some work people and wasn't able to meet her," says Thomas, 35, a finance manager for a car dealership. "When I got home, I told her she was crazy for getting upset—I had already made plans. She just then went off, saying that it wasn't about lunch, but about how she's been feeling like I've been really distant lately. Instead of yelling at me, or even asking me a ton of questions about how I felt about our relationship, she just said what she said and walked off. I felt like I had to defend myself, and her being quiet actually made me start talking. I told her how work was getting me down, how I knew I was stressed and not doing as well as I should be as a husband—stuff I never ever said to her before, even though we've been married for six years."

The point: If you want us to answer questions about what we're feeling, then stop asking about how we're feeling. Instead, watch how we behave, and where our interests lie. And be open about your feelings—the more you show comfort in expressing yourself, the more he'll do the same.

HOW DO I KNOW WHERE THE RELATIONSHIP IS GOING?

I feel like I've hit a snag in a relationship with my boyfriend. We've been seeing each other for a few months. Everything was really great in the beginning. Now, it seems like we've fallen into that typical relationship routine. We see each other during the week, rent a movie on Fridays,

WHAT IT MEANS WHEN

. . . He says "I love you" for the first time (not during sex)

He does. And he thought it long before he ever said it.

. . . He says, "Fine," in response to a question about how his day was

Fine. If something significant happened, he'll tell you—in a few hours.

. . . He says, "Five," when you ask him how many women he's slept with

Twelve.

and usually have sex twice a week (once after the movie). He's nice to me and treats me well, but I'd like to get things back to where they were. He tells me everything's fine, assures me he cares about me, and tells me not to worry about it. But I still do because what he says is one thing but what happens week to week is another. Any idea what he's thinking?

Yeah. He's thinking exactly what he's saying, which is that everything's fine. "Women think that not talking about the relationship means there are problems, but it's the opposite for men. If we're not talking about it, it means we're happy," says Conner, 32. So the real question is not, "What's he thinking?" It's, "What are you thinking?" If you're content with the relationship you've got, then relax and enjoy it. And if you want more, say so. "If a man loves a woman, he'll prove it with daily action not just words," says Jimmy, 27. Either he'll step up to the plate, or what he's giving now is all he's got—and maybe you need to move on.

WHY DON'T GUYS ANSWER EMOTIONAL QUESTIONS?

I've got a good friend who recently left her husband. They have one child who's eight, and my friend and her ex are now in this bitter disagreement about custody, about money, about who gets to see the daughter when. When I told my husband about it, I asked him how he felt about it, because these are really serious issues, and I figured he'd have really serious thoughts on them. Instead, he just sat there, shrugged his shoulders, and said, "That sucks." Does the man have no feelings?

Of course he has feelings, and he told you what they were: He feels the situation sucks.

Oh, but wait . . . you were looking for something more. Here's the problem: You wanted him to tune into your concerns, but the signal you were sending was fuzzier than a pirate radio station. It's the old "feelings" conundrum again. If you want to ask him how he'd handle a custody issue, then ask him how he'd handle a custody issue. If you want to know if he thinks it's wrong for one partner to give up on a marriage, then ask him about that. But don't ask him about his feelings and expect him to surmise that your telling him a story about your friend is some Aesop's fable for your relationship. "We're simple. Please, no hints or assumptions," says D. J., 26. "Say what you mean, mean what you say. Don't make us guess as if we know what you are trying to say or feel."

> **Male Mysteries**
>
> # 65
>
> Percentage of men who don't want their partners to ask more questions about them

D. J.'s a bit of a wishful thinker. Just as men like direct, problem A/ solution B equations, women seem to take a more poetic and metaphorical approach to communication. That's why communication between the sexes is so much work. To men, dealing with hypotheticals is fun when we're talking about football finals and the stock market—not when you're asking us to project how we'd feel about anything really serious, like a breakup or infidelity or pizza toppings. In that case, direct questions will get you the answers you want: let's stay together, I'll be faithful forever, and no anchovies, please.

WHY CAN'T A GUY JUST PLAN OUT OUR FUTURE?

My husband and I have two kids, a boy and a girl, ages three and six. I'm tired of taking the pill, so I've tried talking to my husband about other options. Specifically, I asked him if he wanted more kids. (I could go either way.) And if he didn't, then we should talk about a vasectomy. But he can't decide whether he wants more children, and he doesn't seem too thrilled with the idea of getting the vasectomy. Why doesn't he just tell me what he wants so then we can come up with some kind of game plan?

Your question contains this interesting phrase: "I could go either way." It sounds like you and your husband are both comfortable in a pair of flip-flops. In our polls and surveys, we've asked men about the vasectomy issue.

WONDERING WOMAN

Why is it so hard for guys to write a personal message in a birthday card? Every year all I get is "Love, Jim."

Five minutes on the way back from the newsagent doesn't give a whole lot of time to come up with something clever. Plus, he'd rather let a nice dinner and a show do the talking for him.

John, 41, has been talking about a vasectomy with his wife, but they're having trouble making a decision because they can't get at the root of who really wants to do what. "Neither of us will come right out and say we're done having kids. She thinks me not signing right up for the operation somehow means that I have this evil master plan: that if I dump her, I'll be able to have kids with some 22-year-old bimbo. But I just don't want to get one, because neither of us have closed the door on having kids, and if she's up for it, I'm up for it."

The fact is that men hate admitting that they don't have a plan or a definite opinion either way, and with complex issues like this, it's hard for a guy to decide, unilaterally, the rest of both your lives. He's going to flip and flop like a beached sea bass until he knows for certain what he really wants. And then, one day, he's just going to announce his decision. In the meantime you might want to see if you can figure out what you really want.

I know, it's hard living with us. Just don't try living without us.

MASCULINITY MASTERED: What You Now Know About Men

• Feelings are our F-word. Bleep it out of your conversational repertoire. If you really want to get us talking, try pointed questions like "What do you think about . . . "

• We feel everything's okay when we're not talking about feelings. When we're talking about feelings, we feel everything's on the rocks.

• If you back us into a corner and put pressure on us to communicate, we won't let you into our heads. Give us some space, and we'll let you in.

SAY THIS TONIGHT!

The sexiest thing a woman ever said to Dale, 32:
"What would you like for breakfast?"

The sexiest thing Tricia, 28, ever said to a man:
"I wish I could have you."

Chapter 5

What's Really Bothering Him?

The deep, dark truth about male insecurity,
and why only the woman he
truly loves can make a man feel better.

QUESTION: How often does your wife or girlfriend
compliment you on your body?

Always:............................ 4 PERCENT

Often: .... 19 PERCENT

Sometimes: .... 38 PERCENT

Rarely: .... 24 PERCENT

Never: .... 14 PERCENT

LET ME GUESS. ONE OF THE BIGGEST
complaints you have about the man you're
dating or married to is that he's lacking in the
"just because" department. For birthdays, he
picks up the card and orders the flowers. For
anniversaries, he makes the reservations. For Christmas, he even tries
(albeit in the final hour before the shops close) to pick out a gift that's two
sizes smaller than your normal size. (We're not that stupid, you know.) But
the last time you saw a card, a bunch of flowers or a diamond that had
nothing to do with playing poker "just because" was back when the Spice
Girls were still around.

We know that we're not as generous as we could be with day-to-day romantic gestures like random hugs, compliments, or bunches of wild-flowers picked from the roadside. And we know we need to do better. So don't be shy about dropping the occasional not-so-subtle hint—we'll appreciate it.

But here's the problem: Guys don't drop hints. And we need a little pat on the butt once in a while ourselves.

For you, the flower, card, or occasional "wow, your hair looks hot" works as reassurance that we're happy, we're in love, and that we'd sit through the horrors of a "Friends" marathon if that's what it took to please you. But what guys will never, ever admit—even under threat of torture and/or a forced pedicure—is that we're secretly as insecure as a philanderer at a divorce lawyers' convention.

"We're a lot less confident than you think and need reassurance in our lives as much, if not more, than women do," says Scott, 30, an estate agent.

Less than one in four men say they regularly receive positive reinforcement from the women in their lives, but guys want that reinforcement even more than they want to be in charge of the TV remote. Probably much like you, we don't need gifts to come in an envelope, a vase, or a little light blue box. (Didn't think we paid attention, did you?) Our wish list:

▸*Compliments.* "If you expect me to tell you that you look amazing in the dress you just put on, say the same about me in my suit. Neither of us wear them every day," says Corey, 28. "We wore them so we look good to each other."

▸*Attention.* "A woman can show she cares in many different ways—being taken care of is nice, a dinner in bed, a sponge bath, being talked about highly to other people," says William, 35.

SAY THIS, NOT THAT!

SAY THIS: *Hey, gorgeous!*

NOT: *Hey.*

BECAUSE: *A little part inside of him will actually start glowing.*

SAY THIS: *I love you sooooo much.*

NOT: *Love you.*

BECAUSE: *He needs to know your passion isn't fading.*

SAY THIS: *My God, look at those triceps!*

NOT: *That goes in the kitchen, next to the window.*

BECAUSE: *Home improvement is the closest a guy gets to being an action hero.*

►*Seduction.* Andrew, 32, says, "On Valentine's Day of the first year we were married, my wife called me into the bathroom and she was in the tub with candles and sweets all around. Wow."

►*Recognition of our masculinity.* "We love to hear how strong, wise, insightful, significant, powerful, intellectual, and, most of all, loved we are, over and over and over again. Otherwise, we become paranoid," says Chris, 30.

►*Reinforcement.* "We like to know that we're doing the right thing, even little things like taking out the garbage. A smile, a soft kiss on the cheek or neck, and a thank you will keep us happily doing chores, or anything," says Gary, 34.

You know exactly how it feels when your man offers you one unsolicited, unexpected act of appreciation: It's like putting a magnifying glass under the sun. Everything gets a whole lot warmer. Just because we have an interior more heavily vaulted than a bank safe, that doesn't mean you can't crack us.

So, now, starting today, let's make a pact: more for you, more for us.

WHY DO I HAVE TO NAG HIM TO HELP OUT?

My husband and I both work. The other day, he got home a little earlier than I did, and I was a little frustrated with how the place looked. I got on him a little bit about the fact that the place was a mess and he's got to step up more. He responded by telling me to stop nagging him and that he wished I'd appreciate what he did a little more. What does he want? For me to thank him for managing our stock portfolio and pension fund? It's not like he thanks me every time I send off a bill.

WHAT IT MEANS WHEN

. . . He refuses to discuss the status of your relationship

For him, talking about the relationship is like exposing secret recipes—once you know how it's made, it spoils the mystery and fun of it all. If it's going good, roll with it. If it's going bad, then talk about the specific problem—not "the relationship."

. . . It's been a month of great dates and he hasn't once tried to get you in bed

Start subscribing to bridal magazines. He's got an inkling that you're it.

. . . He asks you to meet his family

He hopes you approach it the way you might a first date—with your irresistible wit, charm, and style. The critics will be preparing to pounce.

WONDERING WOMAN

Three men I've dated have said something along the lines of "If I wanted to be a millionaire, I could be. I'm just not focused on making money right now." Where does this cockiness come from? Is it a facade?

It's the opposite of cockiness—it's insecurity. He's trying to tell you that he knows his job might not be the perfect one to present to your parents, and he knows it might not be the one he'll have in two years. What he's trying to do, actually, is give you information so that you'll have some confidence in him, even if he doesn't himself.

Sometimes, men can feel just as underappreciated as the guy who cleans the gum off the undersides of cafeteria tables. Marc, 35, an insurance agent, says that he works 50 to 60 hours a week while his wife stays home with his three kids (who are all under six). "I know she has a tougher job than I do, but when I come home, I take over and do everything I can to help with the kids," he says. "She views it as part of my responsibility, which it is, but she rarely thanks me for giving her a couple hours' relief—even though I just go from one stressful situation to another." Though it may seem like it, men don't expect a standing ovation every time we walk the rubbish bag out the door or help out with the kids; all we want is the same thing you want for helping to make the family and household run smoother than a fresh shave: A six-letter word, every once in a while.

Male Mysteries

70

Percentage of men who agree that regular compliments directed their way are important

WHAT'S THE PERFECT GIFT FOR A GUY?

I'm stuck. What in the world does a guy want for his birthday? I've been going with this guy for four months, so I have to be careful about not being too mushy, but not being too blah. Have any good ideas?

Hard to say without knowing your boyfriend, but I think guys get off on gifts that are sentimentally practical. What do I mean? The perfect gift isn't one that would register on either end of the romantic extremes (an engraved anything is too ewww, a sweater is too brotherly). So the key is finding something that somehow combines both. Ryan, 32, a lawyer, says, "I do triathlons on the weekend—maybe six or eight every year. For my birthday one year, my girlfriend found some of my old race numbers and photos and she got them all made up in this frame. It was really cool—something I'd never do myself. But now I have it hanging in my office." By the way, when strapped for ideas, birthday sex is always a good last-minute substitute. But it only works if you're into it as much as he is. "The worst sex I've had would be when my girlfriend felt she had to have sex with me because it was my birthday," says Mitch, 25. "Sex should be fun and not an act of going through the motions because it's a special day."

Male Mysteries

34

Percentage of men who say they try their best to change the way his wife or girlfriend wants him to

WHAT DOES IT MEAN WHEN A GUY GOES ON AND ON?

My boyfriend plays in a work football league. I don't really go, because I'm usually working or too tired to get out there. Well, he comes back to my place afterwards—a few beers later, of course—and goes on to tell me about who scored a goal, who got injured, and on and on. It's like play-by-play. It's the most I've ever heard the man talk. How on earth can he spend 20 minutes talking about this and I can't get him to utter three words about our relationship?

You might think that he's fishing for compliments on his athletic prowess. But that's really not the case. What he's fishing for is for you to join him on the boat. He doesn't want to talk about his success; he wants you to see it for yourself. His post-game show is simply his way of indirectly telling you what he really wants—for you to go to a game or two.

MASCULINITY MASTERED: What You Now Know About Men

• Simple compliments about how a man looks will disarm him—and put a smile on his face.

• Men often feel like they're slogging away at life—trying to satisfy bosses, colleagues, friends, family, neighbors, you. One little jolt of acknowledgment that what we're doing is working well helps drive us to slog away some more.

• When in doubt, sex always makes a nice gift. Especially if it comes in fancy wrapping.

SAY THIS TONIGHT!

The sexiest thing a woman ever said to Sam, 34:
"Don't think badly of me, but I love to [bleep]."

The sexiest thing Maya, 24, ever said to a man:
"I want to put you in my wet, hot mouth."
(via text message)

Chapter 6

Why Won't He Open Up about His Feelings?

How men and women deal differently
with emotional pain, and how you alone
can make him whole again.

QUESTION: How often do you think about the woman
who got away?

All the time: . . . . 8 PERCENT

A lot of the time: . . . . 15 PERCENT

Sometimes: . . . . 50 PERCENT

Rarely: . . . . 25 PERCENT

Never: . . . . 2 PERCENT

R EMEMBER THE LAST TIME YOU
went through a breakup? You probably
cried a little, moaned to every friend
who would listen, put on "your" song
and played it endlessly while tearing
pictures of your guy into tiny pieces.

Know what you ex-boyfriend did? Went out and got drunk with his friends, told them all that he was "so over" you, and probably started chasing after some new girl that night.

This behavior explains one of the main differences between men and women—and also explains why, four months later, you've moved on, and he's still drunk-dialing you. ("I wuv yoooo. I mish you shoo much!" Ick.)

Men like to give the impression that they can forget about their former relationships in the time it takes to buy you a tequila shot. But most of us just tuck the baggage under the bed and don't deal with it—until we have to.

Take Jonathan. At 27, he recently went back to college for his master's in social work, and in his first term he met the woman he now refers to as "DG" (for "Dream Girl"). "DG and I were together every second of every day for almost four months," Jonathan says. "Then she tells me she thinks of me as more of a friend. I'm like, 'A friend is someone I buy a case of beer with, not somebody who washes my back in the shower.' Whatever."

To her, Jonathan was cool about it, said he understood. To his friends, he was more messed up than Joan Rivers' lips. He talked about DG constantly, he wondered what he did wrong, he second-guessed himself for not fighting harder to keep her, and he even plotted ways to get her back. (He brought her a single flower on her birthday, three months after they had split, supposedly as a sign of friendship, but really in hopes that she'd realize what a sweet guy he was.) Eventually, he did start dating again, but even after sleeping with two other women, he still found himself talking about DG after a few beers.

Sound familiar? Why are men like this? Men—especially ones who know a good relationship when they have one—tend to remember how

SAY THIS, NOT THAT!

SAY THIS: *Can I start wearing your old football jersey to bed? It's so comfy.*

NOT: *I can't believe you still wear that ratty thing out in public.*

BECAUSE: *That crappy shirt houses 500 precious memories.*

SAY THIS: *She was an idiot to let you slip through her fingers.*

NOT: *Why do you want to talk about your ex?*

BECAUSE: *She's not a threat, so you can afford to be generous.*

SAY THIS: *I want to go to Spain with you and show you all my favorite places.*

NOT: *Let's go to Spain. My ex and I had an amazing time there. It's so romantic!*

BECAUSE: *You want to go to Spain, right?*

much time, energy, patience, and persistence it takes to get the bait, tie the knot, throw in the line, and wait and wait and wait and wait for the right woman to come along. Because we spend so much time trying to catch the next great fish, we often wonder if we already had caught it—and then let it get away.

Male Mysteries

78

Percentage of men who have literally felt "lovesick" (MH)

Does that mean men obsess about their exes? Some men do. (The single most asked relationship question we get at *Men's Health* is this: How do I get her back?) But I think the bigger picture is that you can't assume a man treats the memories of his old relationships like they're Chinese food leftovers—thrown out after a few days. (For Jonathan, it took 18 months and three brief flings before he found the woman to erase DG's memory.) For most men, the surest way to end thoughts about a good ex-relationship is a great next-relationship.

WHY WON'T HE TALK ABOUT HIS EX?

My boyfriend of a few months never talks about his ex, who he went out with for two years, or any past relationships, really. I've asked him what made them break up. He just gives me short B.S. answers, like "we grew apart." Why won't he even talk about it like an adult?

I once dated a woman who did the same thing. She asked me so many questions about my ex-girlfriend I felt like I was on trial for something. She asked me how we met. She asked me what the sex was like. She asked me why we broke up. And every time we went to a new restaurant, she asked, "Did you and *herrrrr* go here, too?" She was acting like a prosecutor in terms of questioning, but I kept mum. Why? Couple of reasons.

WHAT IT MEANS WHEN

. . . He says he wants to take things slow

Things are good. Don't spoil it by constantly asking where the relationship is headed.

. . . He mentions that he ran into his ex

He doesn't want you to worry about what could happen between them in the future. Perhaps feeling like he's not currently being appreciated, he may be trying to remind you that he was in the past.

. . . He stays pretty quiet on a first date

He's banking on the fact that you'll feel curious enough to want to go on a second.

WONDERING WOMAN

Why do so few guys brag about how amazing their wife is? Whether it's at her job or how talented she is at a hobby? It seems like some men don't want to give their wives credit.

Many are uncomfortable bragging about their wives, because they think they'll come off cockier than Tom Cruise and that to their friends they'll look more whipped than the top of a chocolate sundae. It's not right, not fair, and not even smart, but it is what it is.

Because it's not respectful to you, or to our ex, for us to talk about that wild evening in the park fountain. Truth is, yes, we have some great memories of that woman—and if we want to play the highlight reel, we prefer to do it in a private showing. Hint: The less you talk about her and the more you concentrate on us, the quicker we'll forget about the fountain.

WHAT IF A GUY CALLS ME BY HIS EX'S NAME?

One night, my new husband and I were working around the house when he called me by his ex-girlfriend's name—the girl he was seeing just before he met me, more than three years ago. I was shocked, and I know he was flustered. I'm not really that mad, because it wasn't like it was during sex or anything, but still I'm wondering: Is he thinking about her? Is he seeing her? Does he wish that he were with her? Why in the world would that name come up?

One day at work, one of the married guys came in, freaked out. He had called his wife Julia (her name is Jill) when he was leaving for work. "She demanded to know why I called her Julia, so she's thinking I'm either having an affair or interested in someone or flirting or doing something wrong," he told us. So we asked him what the hell happened. He had no idea; he had never even dated a Julia before. Look, men know that there are few greater relationship sins than attaching someone else's name to you (whether it's in bed, at the dinner table, or over at the in-laws'). So if name-slippage does occur, it's most likely linked to some kind of innocent brain-trigger he subconsciously experienced from a TV show, something he read, or just the tiniest thing that could've sparked a fleeting memory of his ex. In reality, if he was actually doing something wrong or if he was longing for his ex, that's the one sin he'd be especially sure of not committing.

DO MEN COMPARE US TO THEIR EXES?

I'm dating a man who was married for three years. He and his ex-wife don't have kids together, but they seem to talk a lot—maybe two or three times every week. And he always seems to bring her up in our conversations. When we were recently fighting about something stupid he brought up some fight he and ex had about something just as stupid. Why does his ex always have to be part of our equation?

In our poll, a guy named Gary, 37, told us that his second wife had a similar issue—and that it caused arguments. "My wife says it's disrespectful for me to even mention my ex's name, even if I'm just trying to bring up a point about what stupid thing she did," Gary says. Gary said that all he was trying to do (perhaps wrongly, since he knows how it bothers his wife) is explain what mistakes he and his ex-wife made before—so that he and his current wife won't make the same ones now. Though I think mentioning an ex's name is the romantic equivalent of dropping ice cubes down your back, some men who talk about their exes do it to say that they're experienced—with women, with conflict, with relationships—and not as a way to say they're unhappy with you.

MASCULINITY MASTERED: What You Now Know About Men

• You are acutely sentimental in short bursts. Men are chronically sentimental in long, painful ways.

• If you have an ex and are thinking about getting back with him, he's probably thinking the same thing. When it comes to breakups, men are weak, weak, weak.

• If you're waiting for him to get over it before you get involved with him, you're making a mistake. All men are on the rebound—that's what we do, we rebound. He's ready to move on.

SAY THIS TONIGHT!

The sexiest thing a woman ever said to Mike, 26:

"No one knows my body like you do."

The sexiest thing Michelle, 32, ever said to a man:

"Lie down!"

WHAT MEN WANT WOMEN TO KNOW ABOUT MEN

"Most women don't realize that men need sex to feel emotionally connected."
—Randy, 33

"Men want to be liked as much as loved. Intimacy is the greatest turn-on. If you share your fantasies and desires, the guy will go to great lengths to please you."
—Wes, 39

"Men like things simple and clear. The more complicated a thing becomes, the less interested a man will be."
—Sammy, 25

"We go to the store to buy some jeans, and we leave with just the jeans. They think that because we didn't buy a new suit, shirt, tie, shoes, and wallet to match our jeans that something is wrong. Women expect men to have the same thought process as they do, and they're wrong."
—Lee, 28

"Even if we're asleep, we're ready for sex."
—Ed, 40

"We wonder why you frequently make us do mental aerobics—asking us hypothetical questions that no man in his right mind would answer truthfully unless he liked getting kicked in the nuts or banished to the couch. Example: Would you ever like to sleep with any of my friends?"
—Ross, 42

"We never get hints."
—Charles, 27

"Men are emotional wrecks; they just don't know how to express themselves."
—Juan, 30

"I cry every time Lois Lane finds out Clark Kent is really Superman."
—Kevin, 32

"The way to a man's heart is to pretend he's still 12."
—Richard, 44

"We need time to play."
—Luke, 34

"Women don't know how insane it drives us when they ask us, 'What are you thinking about?' Sometimes, we're not thinking."
—Leon, 39

"He's probably trying his best. Give him credit for it."
—Seth, 43

"Most of the time, we will do anything we can for you."
—Gary, 38

"If you look at TV shows and commercials, they are just filled with the dumb man scenario. Almost any comedy is about a dumb man who is outsmarted by his women and kids. So men are constantly being told that they don't have to be a smart or thoughtful man; the women will take care of it. Women go into a relationship with no expectations of there being a real man."   —Carter, 45

"Men are always secretly afraid they've done something wrong." —Nelson, 44

"We do dumb things for fun."   —Larry, 28

"A man wants to take care of his woman to the best of his ability. We're a little rough around the edges. That's what a man is—a provider, a protector, a father."   —Evan, 31

"We scratch because it itches."   —Jon, 25

"The remote thing. We don't want to sit there and flip through the channels. It's just that we don't have a choice. See, thousands of years ago, our ancestors were hunter and gatherers. The men were hunters. Their jobs? Run like hell through the woods chasing an animal, which they slaughtered so the family could eat. So we are genetically predisposed to looking at a lot of things, much like running through a forest. We trigger on movement. Women, on the other hand, were gatherers. Their jobs? To walk slowly through the woods and know which of the berries were ripe and safe by judging and comparing colors, smells, sizes. What does it mean? Men are going to like hunting, sports, channel surfing, video games—anything with lots of fast action. Women, who are genetically disposed to compare colors, sizes, and shapes, are going to like to . . . shop."   —Hal, 44

"We're not complicated creatures. The big three for us are food, sex, and sports (not necessarily in that order). Try not to overanalyze everything we say or do. We mostly mean what we say. Just because we look at another woman doesn't mean we're going to sleep with her. We are going to screw up. It's hard for us to say 'I'm sorry.' Give us time and the opportunity to say it in our own way."   —Frank, 38

"I think women just feel love in a more flowery pink kind of way. One night while leaving a cinema, when I was starting to feel sick, my fiancée wrapped her arms around my neck and asked, 'What are you thinking?' I replied, 'I hope I don't puke.' She said, 'Oh, no, that's not the answer I was looking for,' even though she knew how I was feeling. On the way to the car, she was admiring the full moon, thinking I was too, and was expecting me to mention it in a romantic way, but, nope, I was sick."   —Sam, 37

"We don't care if your underwear matches your bra."   —Bill, 27

Chapter 7

How Can I Get Him to Focus on Me?

Why men are far more malleable than you might think, and how to sculpt our rough clay into the hero of your dreams.

QUESTION: Men, what are your favorite sexual fantasies?
(Respondents could pick more than one)

He's a patient, she's a nurse: . . . . 68 PERCENT

He's a student, she's a professor: . . . . 62 PERCENT

He's a professor, she's a student: . . . . 55 PERCENT

He's a patient, she's a doctor: . . . . 52 PERCENT

You're both strangers:. . . . . 50 PERCENT

He's a homeowner, she's a maid: . . . . 49 PERCENT

Granted, early on in our sex lives, we were pretty selfish sexual creatures. Maybe it started when we were teens, when the only woman we had to please was the one in the poster on our bedroom wall, and she didn't demand much from us—no matter what we did, she kept smiling happily. And maybe it continued at university, when our primary focus was figuring out how—and how often—we could score. Now that we're older, though, we redirect our selfishness so that, for many of us, our greatest sexual experiences have less to do with satisfying our bodies than they do with satisfying your bodies— and our egos.

In fact, 49 percent of men say that the best sexual experience they ever had was when they gave a woman physical pleasure beyond her wildest dreams. While we want you to be aggressive, to be creative, and to astound us with your fingers, lips, and toes, we also stake our sexual identity on the fact (uh, hope?) that we can do the same for you.

Take what these men said:

► *"The best sex I ever had was with my current girlfriend, and it was the very first time we did it. We both didn't know what to expect from it, but I knew exactly what I wanted to do to her. She was crazy about the level of attention I devoted to her and my lack of selfishness,"* says Brian, 29.

► *"The best was when I gave her seven orgasms within 30 minutes,"* says Evan, 34.

► *"My main goal in sex is to help you have a great orgasm. I know I'm going to come, so I want to make sure you do as well. In fact, I'd rather give oral than receive. It just turns me on more,"* says Jayson, 30.

► *"It was the second time I had sex with this woman. We both had kids from previous marriages so it was difficult to get away. We took my van to a secluded spot and had a wonderful night. I brought her to four orgasms that night (the most she ever had during a session of sex, she told me). She also was very impressed with how I used my tongue and fingers, on and in her. I must say I was impressed with how she was, too. This was all at the*

SAY THIS, NOT THAT!

SAY THIS: *Let's hang out!*

NOT: *Give me a call if you feel like doing something.*

BECAUSE: *If you're more into it, he'll be more into it.*

SAY THIS: *So how many other women do I have to beat off in order for us to be a couple?*

NOT: *I want us to date exclusively.*

BECAUSE: *Serious conversations don't have to be serious.*

SAY THIS: *Let's scuba dive with giant manta rays in the Maldives next autumn.*

NOT: *Let's go on holiday together.*

BECAUSE: *He won't know he wants to until you start describing it.*

age of 40. Sex after 40 is awesome," says Rick, 42.

► *"I love to perform oral sex on her. I love how she reacts to what I do to her and for her. I always felt I was pleasing her, which made the act so enjoyable,"* says Brock, 29.

► *"We went away on a getaway weekend, had a jacuzzi and a fireplace, and even before we unpacked, I took off all her clothes and leaned her over the back of the couch. With the fire roaring, I kissed all the way down her back, turned her around and did the same thing on her front. I pleased her orally until she had an orgasm,"* says Rudy, 40.

► *"The most beautiful thing to a man is the woman he loves having an orgasm,"* says Matthew, 32

► *"She had me read some early-19th-century erotic literature while she performed oral sex on me. Then she got on top of me and I continued to read until I couldn't take it anymore,"* says Cameron, 29.

Bottom line: We get off when you do.

Of course, our seemingly unselfish side does have a more selfish Jekyll side. By pleasing you, we feel like we solidify our ranking on your list of all-time greats. (You do keep those lists, don't you?) And when we please you, we're anticipating the ultimate reward: reciprocation.

But here's the catch. We know women's bodies aren't like keyboards. We can't press the same buttons in the same order and expect the same kind of results every time. We know that you all react to stimulation in different ways, and we don't always know what you want and what you like in terms of speed, pressure, moisture, duration, and all of the

---

WHAT IT MEANS WHEN

. . . He gets jealous that you're going out with the girls

He's not worried about what you'll do. It kills him that other guys will be looking at you, talking to you, buying your drinks, and wondering what color bra you're wearing.

. . . He can't or won't dance

Dancing feels like public speaking. He hates the potential of looking stupid doing it—especially because you look so good.

. . . He forgets your birthday

He knows he totally screwed himself—and will be doing so for a long time.

WONDERING WOMAN

Why doesn't he go down on me more often?

If you lie back quieter than a library on Friday night, he's not going to know what you make of oral sex. Groan, moan, yell "more," then tell him later that you're dying for a repeat performance. Once you open your mouth about what you like, he'll open his.

other variables that can make you happier than a celebrity at a photo op.

That's why we want you to clue us in.

Terry, 27, was dating a woman for about nine months. In the beginning, they had great sex, but as the relationship went on, he noticed that his girlfriend wasn't into it as much as she once was. So he asked her if he was doing something wrong. "She told me nothing was wrong, that I was doing everything fine, but she wasn't having orgasms the way she once was—or at least the way I thought she was. So I guess I started really questioning whether she was faking in the beginning," he says. "Either I wasn't doing something right at the end of the relationship, or I was never doing it right at all. Either way, I'd like to know. Just please don't fake an orgasm. We can't get it right if you lie about what we're doing wrong."

Truth is, we're good at reading maps. We can get to our destination by looking at signs, using our general sense of direction, and, as you know, without asking for your help. But as much as we've explored your body's topography, we also know that how and where you want to be touched can vary from night to night. So, fine, we're asking for a little help. You don't need to yell, but you can point us to the place you'd like us to travel.

> **Male Mysteries**
> # 71
> Percentage of men who say they wish they could last longer during intercourse *(MH)*

HOW CAN I COACH HIM TO BE BETTER IN BED?

My boyfriend makes love like he's a robot; he's just a little too mechanical. I don't want to tell

**him because I know he'll take it as this big criticism and get upset or
defensive, and I'm sure he'll think I'm this experienced woman who's
slept with all these guys if I tell him exactly the way I like it. How do I
get him to move in the right direction without making him self-
conscious about his skills—or my past?**

You have three choices: One, have an uncomfortable conversation.
Two, remain unsatisfied in your sex life. Both of those options are about
appealing as watching the Brady Bunch grow into middle age: You don't
want to go without enjoying sex to the max, and he doesn't want to hear that
you know exactly what gets you there and it ain't him. But while a verbal
lecture on how to stimulate your body is going to make any man feel
incompetent and embarrassed, we are open to some soft-touch coaching
about your body. Benjamin, 25, a music-store manager, had a girlfriend he
dated for two years. After they broke up and he started dating someone else,
he did the things that always worked for him in the past. "After about the
third time we slept together, she took my hand, moved it down about an
inch, and moaned," he says. "That's all I needed—just a little help in the
right direction." It'll be much easier for him to take directions if you let your
fingers do the talking. Or just give him some breathier hints. "If it feels good,
then give us an oooooh or an aaaaaah. If we don't know that what we are
doing is right or wrong, then we'll keep doing the same thing time after
time," says Louis, 28.

WHAT IF I DON'T ORGASM?
HOW DO I MAKE HIM OKAY WITH IT?

**I just don't have orgasms. Never have. My husband thinks it's a direct
reflection on his ability as a lover. I've tried explaining to him that I love
him, that I wish I could have an orgasm, that it's not him. But it's almost
like he treats sex like it's his mission—that he's determined to stay after
me until I do, which is probably making things worse. How can I let him
know that it's okay to relax and have fun and enjoy it and stop worrying
about my orgasm?**

It's hard to criticize a guy for wanting to please you, but I think you should
tell him that the more he focuses on your orgasm, the more pressure he
puts on you—and the more pressure you feel, the less of everything else
you feel. He needs to relax, and let you relax too. This is going to sound

like a sneaky way to help your husband out, but here's an idea: The next time you're in bed, forbid him from taking any action. Treat his body like it's your mission to please him. Go crazy. Be the aggressor. The point isn't that he deserves more attention than you, or anything like that. The point is that you're trying to relax him so he stops worrying about you and starts to enjoy sex—so you can, too.

HOW CAN I SLOW HIM DOWN— AND SPEED ME UP?

My boyfriend is a little quick sometimes, if you know what I mean. Not like ultra-quick, where it would be some kind of medical condition, but quick as in, I'd like intercourse to last a little longer than it does—and if I'm going to orgasm, I need it to. I mean, I'm flattered and all that he's so excited he can't hold back, but I'd like him to try a little harder. Any suggestions?

Yep: Have sex more often. Or encourage him to take matters into his own hands a few hours before you have sex. "My best sex," says Pedro, 34, "was when we did it twice within the hour and the second time around I lasted a lifetime."

But also remember that some men lack control when they're feeling anxious. Your man may last longer if both of you relax a little, slow down and spend more time selecting music, lighting candles, and going for long, slow foreplay sessions.

> **Male Mysteries**
> # 56
> Percentage of men who say they'll do anything to please their wife or girlfriend

MASCULINITY MASTERED: What You Now Know About Men

• In bed, our priority is making you feel good about sex. One of the side-effects is that it also makes us feel good about ourselves.

• Because our bodies don't work like yours, we need a soft-spoken instruction manual about how you'd like us to flip your switches. Actions speak louder than words.

• The more relaxed a man is, the better he'll perform in bed.

SAY THIS TONIGHT!

The sexiest thing a woman ever said to Barry, 38:

"Let's do this fast so you don't miss the second half of the game."

The sexiest thing Eva, 31, ever said to a man:

"Wow, do that some more."

Chapter 8

What Does His Silence Mean?

Why your man's silence says more
than you think, and how to read his
feelings no matter what his mood.

QUESTION: How often does your wife or girlfriend accuse you of
not listening? (Respondents could choose more than one answer.)

Every day: .... 8 PERCENT

Every time we fight: .... 21 PERCENT

Only when she's upset about something else: .... 28 PERCENT

While I'm flipping the remote as she's talking: . 23 PERCENT

Other times: .... 19 PERCENT

Never: .... 30 PERCENT

ALMOST ONE IN THREE MEN SAY
their significant others never accuse them
of not listening. Then again, maybe they
just weren't listening . . . .

Chances are, you know a handful
of men who are talkers. They talk about anything and everything
without pausing for breath or a moment of quiet before they go onto

the next subject and then they talk some more, sometimes throwing in observations about the last episode of *Lost* and why in the world didn't that goofy kid get kicked off *Big Brother* earlier and on and on and on . . . .

But most of us aren't like that. Most of us keep our lips buttoned and our conversations shorter than a prizefighter's temper. It's not because we didn't hear what you said, and it's not because we're too tired, and it's not because we're too busy following our Fantasy Football team.

It's because we're *careful.*

We know that women are more careful, more intense listeners than men are. So we're very aware that our words have the power to hurt, mislead, madden, or frustrate you, and we want to be sure that whatever it is we're going to say is exactly what we want to say—and exactly what we mean. Sometimes that means we linger over words, and sometimes it means it takes the length of a movie to give you an appropriate response. Better that than the alternative.

"My wife, who is working part-time and raising our kids the rest of the time, once asked me whether I had a feeling one way or the other about her going full-time or quitting and raising the kids full-time," says Todd, 43, a publishing executive. "And I had to think about it. Money wasn't the issue, but I wanted to feel out what she wanted first. If I told her I wanted her to stay home, I knew she'd think that I didn't think her career had value. I ended up telling her that I'd be happy either way, and that she should do what she wants, and that was the truth, but she pushed back, saying that wasn't really much of an answer."

Truth is, a man's not trying to be politically correct or indifferent when he takes time to think about what he's saying; he just knows he's said stupid stuff in the past and doesn't want to make the same mistakes. So when your husband or boyfriend thinks before he

SAY THIS, NOT THAT!

SAY THIS: *Let's hug.*

NOT: *Let's talk.*

BECAUSE: *Most of the time, it works better.*

SAY THIS: *Maybe we should wait and deal with this in an hour or so.*

NOT: *You're not listening to me!*

BECAUSE: *He's not listening because he needs space to think.*

speaks, remember it's probably not because he's not listening well. It's because he knows that you are.

WHY DON'T GUYS GIVE US THEIR HONEST OPINIONS?

One night, I tried on three different outfits and asked my boyfriend which one he liked best. He said he liked them all and that I looked perfect in all of them. He couldn't have been nicer about it, but he didn't give me any help. If he's my boyfriend, I also need him to fulfill some of the "friend" part of that word. I want him to be honest and get an honest opinion. Why do you think he holds back so much?

You say you want him to be your friend, but a guy can fulfill only so many functions without risk of taking some friendly fire. There are just some things he won't be honest about—for his own protection. "I once told my girlfriend that one pair of trousers wasn't all that flattering—I said it a lot nicer than that; I just said the other pair looked better," says Devin, 26. "But she freaked on me, saying that I should love her no matter how she looked or dressed. I tried to explain that I didn't care, but I thought she'd want me to be honest about what she looked like before going out. Uh, no, I guess not." And guys are just more comfortable deferring to their partners on small decisions. As far as the bigger question about him deferring to you on every decision, it's likely he either feels he doesn't have a say, or that if he doesn't have strong opinions about something he'd prefer that you take the lead if you do. "I joke about it all the time with my married friends—whenever there's some relatively minor decision to be made, our opinion counts about as much as the grass's," says Ray, 35. If you want him to open up and let you know what he *really* thinks, you have to give him the key that makes him feel he can unlock his cuffs.

WHAT IT MEANS WHEN

. . . He grunts during sex
When you start hearing jungle-animal imitations, it's a sign that he's turned a corner emotionally— that he trusts you enough not to care about keeping his sex-related noises on low volume.

. . . He grunts during the game
The game has come down to penalties. Please wait to talk about paint colors until it's over.

. . . He says, "nothing," when you ask him what's wrong
He's got four deadlines, a jerk boss, he's frustrated that he's gained weight, and he's freaking out because he can't figure out why the wireless connection on his laptop isn't working. But he doesn't want to talk about it (or anything else), until he clears two-thirds of his problems first.

WONDERING WOMAN

When we started dating he was so social, now he just wants to hit the couch every night. How come?

When a car reaches 90,000 miles, it's probably been through some rough roads. At that point, it needs some time in the garage.

WHY DO GUYS ACT LIKE WEASELS WHEN THEY KNOW THEY'RE WRONG?

A while back, my husband and I had a big fight about whose family we were going to spend Christmas with. He ended up calling my mother a controlling bitch, and we ended up not talking. So instead of just apologizing to me the next day, he wrote me an e-mail saying he was sorry, but then going on and explaining what he really meant. It was nice he apologized, but it was pretty cowardly that he did it over e-mail, don't you think? I think he should have the guts—and another part of the body—to apologize to my face.

Before we focus on what you think he did wrong, let's talk about the good things that happened here. For one, your husband apologized and admitted he was wrong. More importantly, he took the time to write out exactly how he felt. Yes, he should be able to talk it through, but if you were mad, maybe he felt like he couldn't say what he wanted to say without feeling like he was going to be muted. And let's not assume that his e-mail was just a way to dismiss the conflict and end the discussion. Maybe it was just his way of calming both of you down—so you could start it.

WHAT DOES IT MEAN WHEN HE'S NOT ANSWERING ME?

I came home from work one night and told my boyfriend about the rumor that my company might be laying off a dozen people. And then I asked him, "Do you think I need to be worried?" And then there was this long pause. I said, "Did you even hear what I said?" It seems like this happens a lot—like he's not really listening when I try to talk about important things. Sometimes, it doesn't even seem like a conversation. I talk, then wait, talk, then wait. Please tell me that he's not as uninterested as it seems.

When you present a problem or a situation like this, here's how his neurons fire: He balances three competing thoughts: What he wants to say, what you want to hear, and what he thinks you may need to hear. Sometimes, they're the same, and sometimes they're not. So if he pauses for more than a few seconds, it's not necessarily because he's got one eye on the TV and one eye on the microwave clock. "Sometimes, I don't know whether I'm supposed to tell her not to worry about things, or to tell her how I think she should handle the problem," says Zachary, 36. "I try being both supportive and being helpful, but they're not always the same thing." Our male instinct is to try to solve the problem, but we also know from experience that you would rather talk things out than have us dictate a battle plan. Somehow, we're trying to cook up the right combination of both.

Male Mysteries

88

Percentage of men who say they have no clue about the way women think or act

MASCULINITY MASTERED:
What You Now Know About Men

• Silence doesn't equal insincerity.

• When responding to an issue, a question, or a criticism, we craft a response that won't hurt you. Or us.

• Don't long for a man who will chatter more than a hula dancer in Alaska. It's better for a man to show that he cares through his actions, not his words.

SAY THIS TONIGHT!

The sexiest thing a woman ever said to Harris, 40:
"Meow."

The sexiest thing Cindy, 31, ever said to a man:
"There's a dark room around the corner."

Chapter 9

What's the Difference Between Flirting and Cheating?

You may be the favorite woman in our lives, but that doesn't mean you're the only one. Here, men confess about their feelings for other women — and what happens when those feelings get out of hand.

QUESTION: Guys, which of the following constitute cheating on a lover or spouse? (Respondents could select more than one.)

A tipsy make-out session and oral sex . . . . **92 PERCENT**

An anonymous hook-up . . . . **89 PERCENT**

A meeting with an online sex-chat pal . . . . **82 PERCENT**

Drinks and dinner with an old flame . . . . **59 PERCENT**

A mobile phone flirtation. . . . . **56 PERCENT**

Drinks after work with an attractive colleague . . **46 PERCENT**

Googling your ex . . . . **20 PERCENT**

O, WE DIDN'T NOTICE HER. YOU mean the one with the tight green shirt, perfect C-cup breasts, low-cut jeans, lacy underwear peeking out the back, with the hair lightly brushing the top of her shoulders, and with a belly so tight that she makes Jessica Simpson look like Homer Simpson? That one? Nope, didn't spot her.

We hate admitting it to you, but you surely know it anyway. Yes, we look at other women. Yes, we like looking at other women. Yes, some women, when we see them, automatically become filed in our all-time close-our-eyes fantasy file. Nearly four in five men admit to fantasizing about other women while they're in a relationship. Want details? Well then, 18 percent of us fantasize about someone famous, 30 percent about someone we see around but don't really know, 28 percent about a friend or acquaintance, and 14 percent about a past girlfriend.

But here's the thing. We love *you*.

In your mind, it might be impossible to see how we can separate our eyes from our actions, or our eyes from our feelings. In your mind, maybe you think that what we do when we look at other women, think about other women, or talk with other women has to be some kind of a message about our relationship with you. If we look, we must not be happy. If we briefly wonder what another woman looks like naked, we must not be satisfied with you. If we somehow click with the female bartender, then we must be on the next train heading out of Commitmentville. But for us, it's easy to separate. Most times, one has very little to do with the other. We separate the other women in our lives from you, the way we can separate David Hasselhoff from Jack Nicholson. There's only one we really take seriously. See what the men in our survey said:

> ▶ "*We think about having sex with your sister, cousin, aunt, the coffee barista, that chunky woman next to you on the treadmill, but we don't act on it. But we do think about it,*" says Rodger, 39.

SAY THIS, NOT THAT!

SAY THIS: *There are some gorgeous people here, aren't there?*

NOT: *Were you just staring at that girl?*

BECAUSE: *Everyone looks at attractive people, including you.*

SAY THIS: *Seems like Miss So-and-So has a crush on you. I guess I can't blame her. But you're mine, all mine!*

NOT: *I saw the way she was smiling at you. What's that all about?*

BECAUSE: *He's deserves the benefit of the doubt. And if you act playfully competitive, it's sexy. If you act insanely jealous, it's ugly.*

SAY THIS: *Your relationship with her makes me uncomfortable.*

NOT: *Is that bimbo going to be there?*

BECAUSE: *If you explain the specific behaviors that make you uncomfortable, he can stop doing them.*

► *"We have two sides—the committed husband/ boyfriend and the 'check out the hottie' side. In men, the committed wins out, but the checker always exists,"* says Richard, 28.

► *"Thinking about sex and checking out women isn't something we can always control. It comes from the reptile part of the brain—it's a basic, powerful drive. There are times we wish we could stop it; it would make our lives a lot easier,"* says Darin, 30.

► *"It's hardwired for men to look at other women, even though we're as faithful as a golden retriever,"* says Mike, 33.

Throughout our day, we may interact with a dozen different women, and they all may give us different things. A female colleague may fill the need we have for someone to truly understand what's bothering us at work. A female intern may give us the satisfaction of feeling needed (by giving us the opportunity to pass along what we know, that's all). A flirty female waitress may give us that jolt of unsolicited attention we haven't had in a while. Our female hairdresser may give us a moment (albeit a paid-for moment) of feeling pampered. Does that mean we're two minutes away from trying to whisk them off to the Bounce House Hotel? Hardly.

Male Mysteries

47

Percentage of men who think one-night stands are degrading *(MH)*

Keith, 39, a management consultant, has been married for seven years, and he admits he looks at other women, even flirts with them if he has the opportunity. But he's never cheated—and says he'd never even consider it. "My friends always wonder how I can be so friendly and flirtatious with other women, but in my mind, there's not even a question about me cheating on my wife," he says. "I may think about what it would be like to be with another woman, but I

WHAT IT MEANS WHEN

. . . He flirts with another woman in front of you

Believing you take him for granted, he's trying to hint that he has other options if he wants them. He doesn't want them, but he wants you to know that he has them nonetheless.

. . . He looks at other women

He's got a good, strong pulse.

. . . He tips 25 percent to a cute waitress

Good service is worth a tip. Art appreciation is worth a little extra.

don't dwell on it, and when it comes down to it, I don't have the desire to ruin my marriage and family for that."

Of course, some guys are going to cheat, just as some women will. And the danger lies, really, where innocent interactions morph into guilty actions. My point isn't that guys won't cheat; it's that many men feel like they're cut off from other women in their lives because they're viewed as potential threats, potential mistresses, and potential home wreckers. Truth is, what they really give us—whether it's in a few minutes at work or a few seconds as they cross the street in front of our car—is nothing compared to what we hope to get out of being with you.

WHEN SHOULD I BE JEALOUS OF HIS FEMALE "WORK BUDDIES"?

My boyfriend works in an office that's about 75 percent female. I know he has a few guy friends at work, but whenever I ask him who he went out to lunch with, it seems like it's the same three or four chicks that always come up. I try not to be jealous, but I have to admit that I'm not too into the fact that he's spending work time—and non–work time, if you consider lunch, happy hours, and office parties—with that many women. He says they're just friends and that he has no interest in anybody else. How do I know if that's true?

Your jealousy may be grounded, so I'm not going to tell you that you have nothing to worry about. Hell, I'd be jealous if my girlfriend worked in an office full of drooling sharks, and let's face it, the workplace is where a lot of men and women bond over bad bosses, bad coffee, and good gossip. That doesn't mean that he wants to show every woman he works with the inside of a supply closet. Trent, 31, an advertising executive, works in an office with a lot of cute women, and he works very closely with one of them. "My wife, after she met all of them at a work function, really got jealous," he says. "She asked me why I never talked about these women, especially my partner on projects. I never did, because I figured that talking about them would make her jealous—but it actually made her suspicious. Now, I talk about them just as I would any of the guys I work with." That's really one of the ways to judge whether he's keeping his stapler to himself. While he

Male Mysteries

21

Percentage of men who say they secretly love their platonic friend may be reluctant to talk about other women, the real insight comes from seeing how he reacts when you're all together. Does he introduce you to them? Do you all talk, or does one of these women seem to keep her distance when you're around? If he seems to be open about you getting to know them better, chances are he's not trying to do the same.

WHEN SHOULD I BE JEALOUS ABOUT HIS EX?

I live with my boyfriend, so we use the same computer. Once, when I logged in after him, he had left his inbox open. I didn't read his messages, but I saw the names of one or two women that I knew he went to college with. I really want to respect his privacy, but he's never mentioned that he's been in touch with these girls. I don't want to be paranoid, but I don't want to be taken for a fool. If I confronted him about it, I'm sure he'd say the typical things—that it's no big deal, that they got in touch with him, that he loves me, blah blah blah. What's the real story?

Ever watch a guy at the ocean? Some of them run right in—they jump over waves, dive in, and go headfirst. Other guys walk in slowly, checking the temperature, and get in a little bit at a time. Sometimes, they go all the way in, and sometimes, they back all the way out. When it comes to other women, some guys just want to put their toes in—nothing more—with no intention of going in all the way. "Once, I tried to track down the e-mail of someone I had a crush on at school. I found it, and sent her a 'hey, how you doing' note," says Christopher, 34, a married hotel manager. "She wrote back and we exchanged a few e-mails, but that was it. It wasn't like I was trying to get anywhere. I just had this urge to see if I could find her and get in touch

HE SAID . . .

How often men look at other women when they're with wives or girlfriends

If the opening's there, I'll take it:	53 percent
Only in extreme cases, or if wearing sunglasses:	28 percent
Never, I'd like to keep my parts properly attached:	19 percent

WONDERING WOMAN

I know Charlize Theron is hot. He knows she's hot. So why does he have to make animal noises when she shows up on TV?

He's not quite sure how it's different from you saying mm-hmm *every time someone shows a George Clooney clip. Nevertheless, his harmless grunts at Charlize (and Scarlett, Heidi, Halle, Angelina, and Eva) are like burps after a soft drink. He can stop them if he has to, but they're still spontaneous reactions that are hard to control.*

with her." Christopher says he never told his wife, explaining that he didn't feel like he was cheating, but he also didn't think she'd understand what he was doing—and that she'd be really offended by what he did. I can't tell you whether your boyfriend is dipping his toes or diving headfirst into a wave of infidelity, but you did the right thing—respecting his privacy. Since you didn't open any messages, I think you have every right to say what you saw. If he's not doing anything wrong, then there's no harm. But if he is, he'll also know that you're onto him—and he's going to need more than David Hasselhoff to save his ass.

WHEN SHOULD I BE JEALOUS OF HIS PORN STASH?

I found my boyfriend's porn stash. Nothing too hard-core, but it still bothered me. We have a good sex life, and I'm not naïve enough to think that he doesn't do his own thing every once in a while. What does a guy's porn collection say about him—or, more important, what does it say about me?

The only thing it says about him is that he's like every other guy. He likes—brace yourself for this one—breasts. "I keep a small collection of porn—a few magazines and DVDs," says Dean, 37. "My wife travels on business and I'll look at it when she's away. She doesn't know about it, because I'm sure she'd assume that I wasn't attracted to her, which is not true. Just sometimes, to be blunt about it, you need to see other naked women." Porn says nothing about you or your relationship. It's not a slap in your face. It's not a wish-you-could-do-this message. It's not a plea for you to inflate your breasts to the size of hot air balloons. For times when you're away or not in the mood or running to the shop, porn is simply sexual caffeine—a kick-start to get a little jolt going.

MASCULINITY MASTERED:
What You Now Know About Men

• Not all "other" women are threats to the relationship. We *can* be friends with women, even if we've visualized them naked. We can talk to them without wishing their lips were doing something else.

• When we see a beautiful woman, we may not, cannot, or will not (take your pick) avert our eyes.

• Appreciating the beauty of other women does not reflect—or take away from—how we feel about you. There's enough drool to go around.

SAY THIS TONIGHT!

The sexiest thing a woman ever said to Jorge, 26:
"Don't make me wait."

The sexiest thing Sarah, 36, ever said to a man:
"Meet me in the bathroom in 2 minutes."

Chapter 10

Why Do Guys Cheat?

How you can keep him from straying.

QUESTION: Guys, if your partner gave you permission to have sex with someone else, would you?

Definitely would: . . . . 20 PERCENT

Probably would: . . . . 10 PERCENT

Probably would NOT: . . . . 33 PERCENT

Definitely would NOT: . . . . 37 PERCENT

O MATTER WHAT AISLE OF THE supermarket checkout you're in, you can't escape the searing scandals about married men taking up with another woman. There's Jude Law, planting his flag and claiming his nanny for England. There's Brad Pitt, jettisoning everybody's girl next door for a pillow-lipped action figure. Everywhere you turn, some guy is getting caught in a seedy tryst with a seedy triscuit.

All of this extracurricular activity makes no sense when you look at what men told us in our polls. If men are so desperate for the next blonde thing, why do seven out of ten say they'd probably or definitely turn down the chance to parallel-park with a new partner, even if their wife or girlfriend

sanctioned it? How does that account for the commonly accepted theory that 50 percent of men reportedly cheat on their wives, one in six men are cheating on their girlfriend today, and 13 percent of men have even had sex with a friend's significant other?

Good question.

Some men rationalize it by saying they don't want to cheat, but they're slaves to their own biology. "That's the way our genetics work. Historically, men are supposed to spread their seed to as many women as they can to make sure the species stays alive," says Richard, 42. "That's not to say we can't control our actions, but I think there's a pretty big clash between our morality and our biology."

But if you erase the anthropological argument (which I'm sure you already have), I think you'll find that men cheat for the very same reason that women do: They're looking for something they're not getting—or no longer getting—at home.

Remember, statistically, more men admit to cheating than admit to wanting sex with another partner. The logical conclusion, then, is that cheating for men isn't as much about the sex, as it is about what comes with it.

"I was married for four years when I cheated on my wife. It was with someone at work," says Douglas, 37, who's now divorced. "I didn't intend to cheat, and it wasn't like she had a model's body or anything. She was just really flirtatious. She gave lots of attention, told me how much she wanted me, and really made me feel like a god. It's hard to resist that when you go home and the only thing you talk about at home are bills and when I'm planning on cutting the grass."

As you saw from our poll question, men really don't want to sleep around. We don't intend

---

SAY THIS, NOT THAT!

SAY THIS: *I just sent you a naughty e-mail!*

NOT: *Who are you e-mailing at 11 p.m.?*

BECAUSE: *Guys e-mail because it's fun. So have fun with it.*

SAY THIS: *I know you'd never cheat on me.*

NOT: *You promise you'll never cheat on me?*

BECAUSE: *Your confidence helps fuel his fidelity.*

SAY THIS: *Let's talk about the sociology of strip clubs.*

NOT: *You're a pig for going to a strip club!*

BECAUSE: *Everyone gets defensive when they're under attack.*

to hurt the women we're with. We know, logically, that the result isn't worth the action. And we don't condone it. (At least, most of us don't: Only 14 percent of men—apparently still living in that long-ago seed-spreading era—say that it's okay for a married man to cheat on his wife.) From what I've seen, I think more and more men fall into the following category:

"I've certainly thought about other women being naked, and I've always thought about what it would be like to have sex with other women—women I know, women I see on the street, doesn't matter. But I don't act on it, and never have. And I can't see myself ever acting on it," says Brandon, 39, who's been married for eight years. "I've seen too many guys whose marriages have been ruined because of a stupid mistake they made. And I say to myself, why? Why ruin it?"

And yet, ruin it we often do. So I think the real question is what—besides his own guilt, self-control, and loyalty—can stop a man from cheating?

Well, let me ask you a question: What inspires a woman to cheat? Is it because she feels underappreciated at home? Because her life—sexually and otherwise—is in a rut? Because she wants excitement, adventure, even danger? Or maybe because she wants an ego boost, something to tell her she's not older, less attractive, less vibrant that she was on her wedding day?

Exactly. And when it comes to infidelity, men and women are more alike than they are different.

So the best way to ensure a man doesn't stray isn't by monitoring his e-mail or asking the local strip club to issue a restraining order against him or super-gluing his submarine to his home port. It's to treat him the

WHAT IT MEANS WHEN

. . . He goes to a strip club
Live naked women are live naked women. He likes live naked women. He likes looking at lots of live naked women. As artificial, fleeting, and ultimately meaningless as it is.

. . . He says, "nothing," when you ask him what happened at the stag party
He bought four lap dances for the groom, and one or two for himself, most likely with women of a completely different build, race, shape, and hair color to you—just as a harmless fantasy, not as an indictment or reflection of what he thinks about you.

. . . He buys himself new underwear
It's not the universal symbol of infidelity. The man needs new underwear.

same way you'd want—no, need—to be treated if you were tempted to cheat. The way to turn a lover's bow away from the iceberg before it's too late is to look for signs that he needs more attentiveness: more hugs, more kissing, more flattery, more romance. Men crave the chase, the unpredictability, the thrill, the attention, and we want our egos to be stroked as much as any other body part. *All the things that we got in the beginning of the relationship.* As Mike, 43, says, we do know that it's as much our job as it is yours to keep things interesting. "I've always believed that if two people are fully committed to each other, then sexual intimacy is the bond that will keep both from straying away or falling out of love for one another," he says.

Bottom line in all of this: We know why Amazon and pizza delivery have worked so well. All things being equal, it's a lot better to get something great if you don't have to leave your house to get it.

WAS THE SEX REALLY WORTH IT TO HIM TO RUIN EVERYTHING WE HAD?

My husband of five years just admitted to me that he had an affair. He said he slept with a woman he met through a mutual friend at work. He said he only slept with her three times and then they broke it off. Yeah, "only" three times, like I should be thankful or something. To tell you the truth, I don't even know what I'm going to do, if I'm going to stay with him or not. But what I keep asking myself is, is the sex really that much better that it's worth a divorce, splitting up money, lawyers, messing with kids' lives, and all that?

While sex might not be the initial thing that ignites infidelities, it can certainly be a powerful accelerator. "Women underestimate the power of a man's orgasm. We're never thinking about the last one. We're always thinking about the next one," says Ed, 30. If a man needs more sex than he's getting, then his natural reaction is to find ways to fill the tank. First, he tries to fill it with the woman he's in a relationship with, and then he probably tries to fill it more often by himself in the shower. But if he can't get satisfaction from either course of action (physically, in the first case, or emotionally, in the second), then maybe that's when he turns on his radar for outside opportunities. "When I messed around, I know it was wrong, and I know I hurt my girlfriend. The sex was great, but not that much better than with my girlfriend," says Jacob, 26. So, no, men know that the sex isn't worth the mess that cheating can create. But maybe, for some guys, the excitement, the sweat, the urgency, and the attention are.

WHERE'S THE LINE?

I have a friend who broke up with her boyfriend because she caught him kissing a girl at a bar when they were both drunk. It brought up this whole debate between me and my boyfriend about what constitutes cheating. He was saying how he could see that a drunken kiss was just a mistake and not an infidelity, but I didn't buy it. Where do guys view the fidelity and infidelity line?

As you read in the previous chapter, this area has more gray in it than a London sky. Luckily, there are a few no-brainers. Nearly all men view sex, receiving oral sex, and heavy touching as cheating. But things get much murkier after you get through anything involving active body parts. Half of men think that visiting a strip club is cheating, and 20 percent of men say that Googling your ex constitutes cheating. It's one thing when there's a clear-cut case of an affair, but it's another when the two of you don't agree with who crossed what line. "After a party one night, I was the last one there with a girl who was a friend of mine. I was seeing somebody else at the time. We were drunk, but not hammered. She offered to rub my back under my shirt, and then she moved her hands to my chest and said, 'You can do the same to me,'" says Jay, 29. "Oh man, it was tempting, but I didn't and I left. I know I did the right thing, but there's no doubt in my mind that my girlfriend would think I did something wrong because I let her touch me and I put myself in a pretty bad position. So I never told her, because I stopped things before anything happened and I don't think it was cheating." The line varies greatly among men, which is why you might want to parse out each other's expectations early on in the relationship, and define what, exactly, "exclusive" really means. But I think most guys view the line like this: Men think they're cheating if they actively do something physical involving mouths or genitals to or with another woman. Therefore, flirting or dancing with other women, watching porn, going to strip clubs, even sending questionable e-mails don't constitute cheating in the minds of many men.

> **Male Mysteries**
>
> **40**
>
> Percentage of men who feel justified having an affair if their wife had one first *(MH)*

WONDERING WOMAN

Why does it turn him on so much to see something he's not supposed to—like a woman's nipples through her shirt or a flash of panties as a woman is going up the stairs?

No matter how many times he's seen them since, he'll always have a soft (and hard) spot for the forbidden grails he lusted after as a hormonally electrified teen.

And that's why, if you think differently, you need to tell him early—so he can agree, argue, or even leave the relationship. Better you disagree *before* something happens than after.

WHY'S HE LOOKING ONLINE?

I found out that my husband has an online dating profile. He lied about his age, his marital status, and he even goes on about what he's looking for. When I confronted him on it, he said he's just playing around—that he never intended to do anything. But even if I buy that (and believe me, I don't), I don't understand how he thought he wouldn't get caught. Are guys just stupid when it comes to this cyber stuff? There's a part of me that even understands how a man can fall for a colleague, but here, it's like these men are actively seeking opportunities to cheat. Why?

Because a lot of men feel about as secure as a box of chocolates in the middle of a Weight Watchers meeting. Men may put up an air of confidence, but when it comes right down to it, we're not so sure about our looks, our bodies, our careers, or anything else. So what do we do? We go to a very controlled setting (the computer), rather than a very unpredictable and vulnerable one (the bar). "I put up a profile to see how people would respond, even though I knew it was wrong because I was married," says Lawrence, 39. "But then it just sort of became addictive, like I wondered how many more women I could contact, and how much more attractive they could get. I know it's wrong so I stopped it, but I think it's the idea that online dating is like a buffet—there are so many possibilities that you never run out of options and you're always pushing yourself to see if you can get more of it." Some stats show that 20 percent of unavailable men go online and say they're available. It's not because they think they'll never get caught. It's because they think they'll never get caught *up*—they can troll the waters without ever actually setting the hook. The bad news is, they're probably wrong—in both cases.

MASCULINITY MASTERED:
What You Now Know About Men

• For men, cheating isn't always about sex. It's about all the excitement, romance, danger, and intrigue that surround it.

• Men don't want to cheat. They want to be faithful. They want to be loyal. They want to be considered a good man. They'd prefer it if you—not another woman—made them feel that way.

• Temptation can be as controlling and action-altering as any drug. Detox isn't the answer. Helping him indulge, revel, and experience it at home may very well be.

SAY THIS TONIGHT!

The sexiest thing a woman ever said to Randy, 29:

"I'm going to make you forget about anyone else you've ever been with."

The sexiest thing Lindsey, 26, ever said to a man:

"Close your eyes. And try not to make any noise."

Chapter 11

Are Men as Vain as Women?

Why men are terrified of mirrors,
and how you can use those fears to build
him up — or break him down.

QUESTION: Guys, what's the one thing you'd most
like to change about your appearance?

Gut: . . . . 42 PERCENT

Hair: . . . . 8 PERCENT

Chest: . . . . 6 PERCENT

Penis: . . . . 8 PERCENT

Face: . . . . 7 PERCENT

Other: . . . . 18 PERCENT

Nothing: . . . . .11 PERCENT

O MATTER HOW OFTEN YOU FIND
us standing by the door, tapping our feet,
and looking impatiently at our watch,
the fact is we appreciate all you do to
look good: the makeup, the hair, the
waxings, the nails, the moisturizers. And it certainly doesn't help when the
Victoria Beckhams of the world seem to be telling you that beauty is about
being thin enough to hide under an Oriental rug.

So I'm sure you look at us with a loofah full of resentment and think we've got it easy. If we don't want to shave three days in a row, it's our rugged look. If we skip the shower on a Saturday morning, we can just cover up our hair with a cap. And when summer rolls around, well, it's not like our bathing suits are the size of three poker chips.

But here's our dirty little secret: Men like to come off as if they care about their appearance as little as they care about anything featured in Cosmopolitan, but the truth is that we have plenty of body-image issues of our own. (We don't sell 24 million copies of *Men's Health* magazine every year because guys *don't* care about how they look.) It's just that deep in the recesses of the Unspoken Male Code, right between "Scoff at diet soft drinks" and "Be wary of anything purple unless it's in a sports team's logo" is one very important rule: "Never admit you're worried about how you look." So you're not going to hear us ask if these jeans make our ass look big, or if our back hair is getting too Kong-like, or if that flabby jiggle hanging over our belts is something we should be concerned about. We're afraid that you'll label us as too vain, too weak, too metro, too feminine, too devoid of the confidence you want and expect in a man.

But the thing is, while we don't want to talk about our bodies, we wouldn't mind if you did.

Just a little.

Patrick, 38, a financial analyst, steadily gained about 20 pounds in the first five years of marriage. "I just felt kinda gross, having to wear shirts at the beach and buying bigger clothes, but never talked about it. My wife never brought up my weight either, so I don't know if she cared or if she just didn't want to say anything because she thought it would bother me," he says. But a week after he started going back to the gym and eating better, his wife told Patrick as he was leaving

---

SAY THIS, NOT THAT!

SAY THIS: *You look fantastic.*

NOT: *It's good to see you.*

BECAUSE: *He needs to hear it.*

SAY THIS: *We should go to the gym.*

NOT: *You should go to the gym.*

BECAUSE: *His ego is as tender as his flabby abs.*

SAY THIS: *Hey, I'm waxing my legs tonight, want me to wax your shoulders at the same time?*

NOT: *Your shoulder hair is gross.*

BECAUSE: *If you make it out to be no big deal, he'll jump at the chance.*

for work that his trousers looked looser and his gut looked a little smaller. "You don't understand. Usually the only time my wife talks about how I look is if I have wing sauce dripping down my chin," he says. "I knew that a week wasn't enough to have any real big physical effect, but what she said was nice to hear, and it made me want to do even better."

Now, we get praise from bosses and a "nice garden" from the neighbors, and those words of encouragement make us want to keep up the good work. The same kind of positive feedback from you would go a long way. "We're just as insecure as women, if not worse, but we just don't show it," says Mitchell, 31. "We need compliments, too, and to be told we're attractive." After all, if you're going to spend so much time making yourself look good, it's only fair that the man at your side do his part as well. All it takes is a little inspiration from you.

WHY CAN'T GUYS JUST ACCEPT THEY'RE BALDING AND BE COOL ABOUT IT?

There's a new guy who started at work, and he's been sending me signals. I'd say he's in his early thirties, and he's losing his hair—receding in the front and also a little from the top. That's fine, but here's the thing: He grows the front of his hair really long and then brushes it straight back to cover the back bald spot. And it looks, well, kind of ridiculous. Why doesn't he see that by trying to hide it, he's really announcing to everyone how insecure he is?

Reminds me of a man I saw when I was getting a haircut a few months back. He was bald, except on the sides, and when he sat down in the chair, he kidded with the stylist, "A little off the top, please." Men deal with baldness—and all body issues, really—in two ways. We either try to hide the so-called flaw (as in the case of the guy at your work) or we turn our flaw into our comedic sidekick (like the guy I saw). While we know that hair loss has nothing to do with whether we're funny or good in bed or talented in our jobs, men also view losing their hair as one of the most emotional breakups they'll ever go through. Michael, who's 29, says, "I'm starting to lose my hair. I really admire the guys who can shave their heads when they do, but I'm not ready to do that and I don't think I can pull it off." That phrase—*pull it off*—hits at the very heart of our insecurities. We all have something we don't like about the way we look, but the issue is

WHAT IT MEANS WHEN

. . . He grooms/trims/waxes his body hair
The perfectly groomed man is simply trying to send messages to you about his personality: cool and polished, and therefore desirable.

. . . He rarely grooms anything
The imperfectly groomed man is simply trying to send messages to you about his personality: cool and relaxed, and therefore desirable.

. . . He says he's going to start a diet
He's announcing his plans, but it's also code for how he feels: He feels lazy, fat, tired, and about as desirable as a sauceless chicken wing.

which side we take in the confidence spectrum—the side that will do anything to hide it, or the one that feels comfortable outing it.

WHY DO MEN OBSESS ABOUT THE SIZE OF THEIR JOHNSONS?

My boyfriend obsesses—I mean *obsesses*—about the size of his penis. He constantly apologizes, he asks me how he compares to past boyfriends, and I've even caught him checking out Web sites that sell penis-enlargement products. I don't know how many times I have to tell him that he's about average, it's no big deal, he's great, and I don't care what size he is. Why can't he get over it? It's not like anyone else besides me even sees it.

Guys just don't know what "average" is because their perception of penis size comes from an occasional and unintended locker-room glance and from porn films. So even average-sized guys can they think they're stubbier than a Mini Cooper and everyone else is longer than a tractor trailer. Tim, 31, a sales manager, recently broke up with his girlfriend of three years. When he started dating again, he also started worrying about the size of his manhood. "I had been with one woman for so long that I really didn't think about it all that much," he says. "But the first time I had sex with a different woman, I was a little gun-shy about getting undressed. I know I'm smaller than other guys and I couldn't help but wonder what she was thinking." We know the size of the drill isn't supposed to matter as much as the battery-pack that powers it. In fact, three-quarters of women say they are satisfied with their partner's penis size—and that's something you need to let us know. Still, many of us can't help thinking the substance of our manhood is dependent on the size of our manhood, and we can't help but wonder how we

rank among the other males who've vied for—
and won—your attention in the past.

WHAT MAKES A MAN GET HIMSELF IN SHAPE?

My husband has always looked the same way for as long as I can remember him—he wears the same kind of clothes as he did when we were dating, he has the same hair cut he's had for 10 years, and he's always been just a little bit chunkier than he should be. Nice, normal, steady. A few months ago, he changed his hair, bought different clothes, and started working out. He's only 33, so it's a little early for a midlife crisis. Is he having an affair? If not, what's going on? Why now?

Mark, a 42-year-old writer, remembers the reason why he lost weight. His four-year-old daughter said to him, "Dad, are you pregnant?" And that was all he needed. "My wife had nagged me for three or four years to clean up my act, but those four words were all it took," he says. Men don't want to be fixed or lectured or nagged. Instead, we respond to epiphanies—the moments, the comments, the seemingly inconsequential times in life that shake us up and are actually very consequential. Funny thing is, those epiphanies don't need to be negative, like the one directed to Mark. They can come from you noticing—and mentioning—when we look *good* to you. It's all about pushing a small button that turns our desire to change into making a change. I have no idea what exactly is going on with your husband, but don't jump to negative conclusions just because he's changing his appearance. I'd be willing to bet that it was something small that made him want to do something big.

Male Mysteries

60

Percentage of men who aren't satisfied with their penis size

WONDERING WOMAN

Buying new trousers. Is it really so hard?
Yes.

MASCULINITY MASTERED:
What You Now Know About Men

• Men can be as insecure about their bodies and appearance as women. A few well-timed compliments about what you like about our bodies—even if we don't—will win us over. For a long time.

• When it comes to our appearance, you can help us by being a little like a good coach. Push us in the right direction if we need to be pushed, but tell us when we've done something right. We can take a few boos, as long as there's some cheering, too.

• Size does matter. To the guy who owns it.

SAY THIS TONIGHT!

The sexiest thing a woman ever said to Drew, 32:
"Let's do it again."

The sexiest thing Jennifer, 22, ever said to a man:
"I'll take you home and ride you like a Harley down a bumpy road."

Chapter 12

Why Do Men Always Have to "Fix" Things?

If you think he's not attuned to your feelings, you're wrong. Here's why they matter so much — and how you can help each other change for the better.

QUESTION FOR THE WOMEN: Why don't you ask men for advice on relationship problems? (Respondents could choose more than one.)

Men don't understand: .... 19 PERCENT

They can't relate: .... 16 PERCENT

They're poor listeners: .... 15 PERCENT

They never know the right thing to say: .... 12 PERCENT

They don't give good advice: .... 7 PERCENT

They're too busy looking down my shirt: .... 4 PERCENT

Some other reason: .... 34 PERCENT

No reason: .... 25 PERCENT

A FEW MONTHS AGO, DAVIS, A 38-year-old civil engineer, came home to find his wife crying. When he asked Ilana, who works in fundraising for a charity, what was wrong, she told him that that she had just been passed over for a promotion at work, that somebody who didn't deserve it got it, and that she felt like she was stuck in a job where she was unappreciated and underpaid. "I told her she should go in and explain her feelings to her boss. But when she said it was no use, I said she should get her C.V. together because the job was obviously no good for her, and then she just lashed out at me," he says. "She told me that I didn't understand, that it wasn't as easy as picking up and moving, and that I couldn't just come in there and expect she'd stop being upset because I told her to find a new job."

You might not be able to tell it by the job he did on the kitchen tiles, but men like to fix things. It goes for stuff around the house, stuff with wires, stuff in toy boxes, and stuff in your head. And it's one of the things that men in our survey echoed over and over again.

Give us the problem; we'll give you the equal sign.

> ▶ *"Men fix things. Don't come to me for sympathy about problems unless you want them fixed,"* says Timothy, 30.

> ▶ *"If a man hears his woman complain about something, he figures she wants it—whatever it is—fixed. That doesn't seem to always be the case. I wish women would only bring things up that they want us to act on. It would be less confusing for us men,"* says Bruce, 37.

> ▶ *"Men think in terms of facts: men look for solutions to problems and don't think that just listening will solve any complaint,"* says Lee, 24.

> ▶ *"We like to solve problems, so we feel bad when we can't solve yours,"* says Nate, 25.

That's exactly right. We feel bad when we can't fix things for you.

Fifty-three percent of men say that when their girlfriend or wife comes to them with a problem, they typically offer suggestions for solving the problem (that's more than those who say they sympathize and relate, listen, or even pretend to listen). You're wired to give sympathy when people share their problems with you, and maybe that's why you expect it of us, too. Us? We're wired to

SAY THIS, NOT THAT!

SAY THIS: *I need to vent for 10 minutes straight.*

NOT: *I need to talk.*

BECAUSE: *It lets him know that you want him to listen, not contribute.*

SAY THIS: *Thanks for trying to help.*

NOT: *You're not helping*

BECAUSE: *He is trying.*

analyze the problem, dig in, take care of it, and move on to the next one.

It may be that you prefer problem-solving foreplay— hugging, listening, nodding, talking. We like problem-solving quickies—thinking, deciding, acting. "My girlfriend says that I always try to solve her problems, so I tried stopping, but whenever she tells me something and I don't give any solutions, I feel like I'm no help at all," says Jamie, 27.

So when you have a problem that we can't help you resolve—be it an issue at work or a fight with your mother or a health issue that won't go away—it may be frustrating for you that we don't keep our mouths shut, but it's as frustrating for us if we do.

We want to help. We want to solve. We want to fix. And if we can't, then we feel like there's something else that's broken. Us.

HOW DO I GET HIM TO ADDRESS OUR RELATIONSHIP PROBLEMS?

Things haven't been going that great with my boyfriend. I told him how I felt—how I wanted more from our relationship, how I didn't feel like he cared as much as he used to, how it seemed like we were in kind of a rut. His response? He clammed up. He made some remark about how he was sorry I felt that way and then came back with the classic: "What do you want me to do?" I hate that. It's like he was trying to pass the responsibility of the success of the relationship back to me. What's he trying to prove whenever we have relationship troubles?

To you, "What do you want me to do?" may sound like a cop-out or a blow-off. But to us, that question sums up every single emotion we have when it comes to relationship problems. Just tell me what to do. Tell

WHAT IT MEANS WHEN

. . . He hugs you (after a first date)
He wants a second.

. . . He hugs you (after sex)
He's awed by you.

. . . He hugs you (after a fight)
Makeup sex, anyone?

WONDERING WOMAN

Why does he spend three weeks researching even the smallest purchase?

A man can be impulsive about women and beer choices, not about his money.

me how to fix it and I'll try to do it. Tell me how to make you happy. We know—logically—that life isn't a maths equation, that one gesture, behavior, or sentence on our part can't fairy-dust bad feelings into good ones. But that's the way we try to get there. "We think differently than women do," says Luke, 26. "I'm just more linear in my thought patterns. I still want to meet your needs and get to the bottom of what's bothering you. I just drive there differently."

WHY DOES HE TURN EVERYTHING INTO SOMETHING ABOUT HIM?

The other night, I got into a pretty big fight with my mother. We were talking about Christmas and who was going to go where, and she made some remark that I always find a way to ruin them. I was mad and upset, and I told my husband the whole story. Then he went into this long story about when his sister got into a fight with his mother about something when they were kids. I just wanted to unload a little bit and he turned it around so it was all about him and his family. Why couldn't he just listen?

In our poll, about 10 percent of men say they take this tactic—trying to relate their own similar circumstances to your problem. I don't think he's telling you this to negate or dismiss your story; he's giving you background so you can see the solution. "My girlfriend tells me all the time that whenever she tells me a story about herself, I try to top it with one of my own," says Bo, 25. "I'm not trying to top her. I'm just trying to relate to her. I thought that's what she wanted." As for why we don't listen; it's because we think—we feel—that listening to your problem is like slicing a pizza with a paper clip. It's not helping, so why bother? In our minds, we wonder what good it is to you for us to sit there and nod without saying anything if we can't help you find your way out of your maze of stress, unhappiness, or frustration? We feel that if we just listen without making suggestions or telling you about similar problems, you'll think the actual opposite—that we aren't even listening at all.

WHY CAN'T HE BE MORE AFFECTIONATE IN PUBLIC?

There's one couple we're friends with who seem like they have the perfect relationship. They both have great jobs, two really sweet kids, they travel a lot, and they always seem so sweet together. After my husband and I hung out with them one night, I made the comment that they were so cute and seemed really happy. My husband said, "You mean you're not?" And that triggered this whole fight. He said he hated how I compared us to other couples and just because some husbands calls their wives "sweetie" doesn't mean that's what relationships are made of. Why'd it hit such a hot button with him?

Because your husband took your comment as code for: You're an unfeeling lout who gives me none of what a woman deserves. "My girlfriend always says she wishes I'd be more affectionate in public. Nothing big, just more hand-holding and stuff. I just don't like it. She'll even make little comments when we pass people on the street about how cute it is when they do that," says Andre, 34. "The comments seem like no big deal, but it's actually one of the things that really pisses me off about her. It's like here I am, I do a good job at work, treat her well, and think I'm a pretty good boyfriend, but there's one thing I'm not comfortable doing, and now I'm some sort of bad guy who's inferior to every other hand-holding, kiss-giving man in the world." Why does it bother us so much? Besides the fact that we don't like our romantic (or unromantic) personalities to be judged against other couples in a reality-esque competition, we also don't like that you assume another man's answer to a situation is the answer to ours.

Male Mysteries

4

Percentage of men who pretend to listen to a woman's problems, without saying much

MASCULINITY MASTERED:
What You Now Know About Men

• Our instinct is to help. If we only listen to your problem without offering a solution, we feel like you'll think we're not listening at all.

• We're not trying to sweep your problem under the rug. We're trying to get it off your plate.

• If we ask what you want us to do, we always appreciate concrete answers.

SAY THIS TONIGHT!

The sexiest thing a woman ever said to Aidan, 22:
"Your lips know what they're doing."

The sexiest thing Lisa, 29, ever said to a man:
"All women should be this lucky."

Chapter 13

Why Do Men Fear Anger?

There's only one thing a woman can
do to truly make a man fight things out —
and one sure way to calm the savage beast.

QUESTION: Guys, what do you and your mate typically fight
about? (Respondents could choose more than one.)

Money:. . . . . 38 PERCENT

Housework/household responsibilities: . . . . 26 PERCENT

Sex: . . . . 24 PERCENT

That she thinks he takes her for granted: . . . 22 PERCENT

Level of commitment: . . . . 21 PERCENT

She wants him to share his feelings: . . . . 19 PERCENT

Kids:. . . . . 17 PERCENT

How much time he spends at work: . . . . 14 PERCENT

In-laws: . . . . 13 PERCENT

Fidelity/other women: . . . . 9 PERCENT

AST YEAR, GENE, 42, WHO WORKS
for a commercial estate agency, received a
large year-end bonus. On his way home from
work that day, he stopped at the electronics
shop and ordered a big-screen TV.

When he got home and told his wife, she flipped like a Cirque Du Soleil performer. "She went crazy, telling me I had no right to spend the money without talking to her about it. She said she couldn't believe how inconsiderate I was," he says. "So I came right back. I said I never spend anything on myself and it was bonus money, not in our regular budget, and I wanted to treat myself to this one thing because I busted my ass the whole year and I deserved it. We didn't talk to each other for three days and it was a good two weeks before we were finally able to get past it and talk about it normally."

When he looked back, Gene realized that while he may have been right with some points and wrong with others, he was way off in his delivery—and in the fact that he didn't include his wife in the loop before the purchase. "But she came at me swinging axes. If she had just said what she felt without going crazy, it would've saved us a whole lot of bad blood."

Guys hate fighting because we instinctively equate fighting with aggression and anger. So if you want to really engage your man in an argument, the best tactic is to first get your anger under control. When we're confronted directly, our instinct is to become hostile and defensive. Just because it's a verbal assault doesn't mean we react any differently than if it were a physical one. Throw a punch, and our instinct is to throw back.

Or—since we are fight-or-flight creatures— we'll take the other option. We'll retreat.

"If my girlfriend reacts emotionally to a problem, then I just stop talking," says Bryan, 34. "I don't want to talk about anything if she's super angry, and that just makes her madder. It's like that scene in *Top Gun* when the guy who replaces Goose is telling Tom Cruise, 'Engage,

---

SAY THIS, NOT THAT!

SAY THIS: *You have a right to be pissed.*

NOT: *Calm down.*

BECAUSE: *He wants to be validated, not sedated.*

SAY THIS: *I love the way you do this, this, and this, but that bothers me.*

NOT: *That bothers me.*

BECAUSE: *Criticism goes down better with a sugar coating.*

SAY THIS: *Let's take five. I'm sure we both need a break.*

NOT: *You should just go.*

BECAUSE: *Even though you're fighting, he needs to know you're on the same team.*

Maverick! Engage, Maverick!' But Maverick kept saying, 'It's not right, it's not right.' He didn't engage until he was ready, and I'm not going to fight until she calms down."

When you consider that most men either blow up or retreat when confronted, you can see where the problem lies—nothing ever gets talked through. I'm not saying that you shouldn't be emotional and passionate, and I'm not even questioning whether your anger is justified (because it probably is). I'm just saying that if you really want to resolve an issue, then take your emotions out on a tissue or a punching bag—and then take up the issue with him.

Male Mysteries

15

Percentage of men who say they don't fight with their wife or girlfriend

"All I want is for women to understand that men and women are different creatures who see the world from different angles, and women can't get stuck on trying to make the man in your life see things your way," says Max, 34. "One secret to a successful relationship is the couple's ability to amiably agree to disagree."

WHY DO GUYS BACK AWAY FROM FIGHTS?

My boyfriend will not fight. He refuses to, and it's something that really bothers me about him. Every once in a while, I just want him to go back and forth with me, even if it's over something stupid. One time, just to see if I could get him going, I accused him of being extra-flirty with a waitress. He just shrugged it off, told me I was crazy, and wouldn't even defend himself. How can I get him to mix it up a little bit? I think fighting is healthy for a relationship, and he thinks it's destructive.

WHAT IT MEANS WHEN

. . . He clams up during a fight
Could mean two things: One, he doesn't want to say something that will get a toaster thrown at him. Or two, he knows that keeping silent will make you so mad that you'll want to throw a toaster at him.

. . . He says something really mean during a fight
He keeps most emotions bottled up for a long time. If it pops, it pops good.

. . . He gets insanely jealous over ex-boyfriends
The only thing worse than thinking about you naked with another man is thinking about you naked with the man the two of you just ran into at a restaurant.

WONDERING WOMAN

Why won't he just say "I'm sorry"?

Because he's misguided. He thinks that apologizing makes him less of a man, when the reality is the opposite.

Some guys love fighting if they're in a bar or in the ring, but most of us don't like to fight if we're in love. (A small percentage of men even say their fighting style is to deny there's even a problem to begin with.) "I hate fighting. I don't mind disagreeing, but I hate fighting. To me, it feels like a weakness in the relationship if I fight," says David, 28.

Now, I don't think there's any way to turn a relationship pacifist into an H-bomb button-pusher. If a guy doesn't want to mix it up—especially about things he thinks he can work out without fighting—then you're not going to change his style. But really, out of all the issues you could be fighting over, are you sure you want to make the style of fighting one of them?

WHY DO MEN PUT US DOWN SOMETIMES?

My fiancé and I had a pretty big fight about money. We were having that big talk about how we were going to merge bank accounts, how we should allocate savings, who's going to do bills, all that stuff. But then he started to get really sarcastic—saying I couldn't even figure out the tip at restaurants. This is the way he handles all of our fights; he gets really sarcastic. Then if I call him on it, he says he was just trying to be funny. But I think it's really mean and condescending. What does he get out of putting me down?

What he gets is a shield of armor. He figures that if he can make his point with a joke, with a slight, with a minor insult, then maybe he can get a little bit of advantage in the issue. "Trash-talking in sports isn't always malicious. It's just a little way to play mind games to assert yourself as a stronger person than your opponent," says Kevin, 32. "I've seen my friends do it with their wives. Just little jabs here and there—they say it's in fun, but it's really a fighting tactic they use to end the fight."

WHAT'S SO WRONG WITH A LITTLE NAGGING?

Okay, I'll come clean. I know that I nag my husband a little bit. He says I nag him about everything from the way he picks up after himself to the way he leaves the bathroom in the morning. I don't mean to be mean; I just want him to have respect for the things around him and for our house. It's just little stuff, so I don't think of it as that big of a deal. But I always hear guys say they can't stand the "nagging" from their wives and girlfriends. Do guys really have such thin skin?

There are two ways you break a rock. You slam it to the ground and watch it crumble into pieces. Or you chip, and chip, and chip, and chip, and chip away until nothing's left. They both get the same result, but with one of the methods, the pain lasts a whole lot longer. "Nagging doesn't get results. If she would approach me with respect, she would get better results," says Ryan, 27. An easier way to motivate a guy is to play into his problem-solving reward center: Point out how great the bathroom would look if he kept it clean, rather than how bad it looks when he makes a mess. As soon as his brain registers the clean bathroom = happy wife equation, he'll do it.

Male Mysteries

19

Percentage of men who say they fight like a lawyer, trying to trip women up with arguments

MASCULINITY MASTERED: What You Now Know About Men

• Men are scared of anger. The less you show, the more you'll know.

• Many men don't see fighting as the cleansing and relationship-strengthening act that you do. To you, fighting may show emotion. To us, we'd rather explain before it gets to the point of verbal punches.

• Backed into a corner, we fight back ruthlessly or retreat silently. We're fairly sure you prefer neither.

SAY THIS TONIGHT!

The sexiest thing a woman ever said to Bill, 24:

"You're the best thing that's ever happened to me."

The sexiest thing Jessica, 25, ever said to a man:

"Unwrap me!"

Chapter 14

Do Men Believe in Love at First Sight?

Why one little gesture can be the difference between "just friends" and a lifetime of happiness.

QUESTION: Guys, what most attracts you to a new woman?

Looks/physique: . . . . 35 PERCENT

Eye contact: . . . . 21 PERCENT

Smile: . . . . 19 PERCENT

Confidence: . . . . 12 PERCENT

Opening words: . . . . 5 PERCENT

Clothes: . . . . 2 PERCENT

GUYS WANT DATING TO BE LIKE a maze. We'll play mouse, you play cheese. Do we want the cheese? Yeah, more than anything. Can we smell the cheese? Yep. Do we know exactly how we're going to get the cheese? Not a chance. But that doesn't mean we want you to place the cheese right in front of us before we even get out of the start. We want to look, we want to think, we want to figure it all out. Because that makes the cheese a whole lot tastier in the end.

That's not saying we want you to play games, deceive us, lure us in, and then close the door on us in exchange for our faster, wiser, and genetically superior brethren. All we're saying is we like the dating game—and we like the fact that there are few things (besides penalty shoot-outs and prostate exams) that makes us more nervous than finding our way to you.

Fact is, when we're courting, approaching, stalking, or just trying to get to know you, we've got more butterflies than a Costa Rican guidebook. For us, our early nervousness stems from wondering if we're rusty, prepared, or able to perform. And this audience—you—is a hell of a lot more intimidating than any other we've faced.

But here's the thing: If we're interested in you in the long term, we don't want you to ease all of our anxieties with a proclamation of love or even an invite to the bedroom. At least, not right away.

> ► "A woman who teases on the first date is so sexy. Just enough to let us know that she's interested, but not so much that she looks desperate," says Danny, 32.

> ► "I'm all for women being aggressive— I wish more of them would be. But they have to know where to stop. The woman who touches me, brushes up against me, and does stuff like that early on is much more long-term material than the woman who jams her tongue down my throat after 30 minutes," says Allen, 36.

> ► "The sexiest thing a woman did to me was when I first met her at the bar: She just took her hand and hooked two fingers into my front trouser pocket when she was talking to me. Holy crap. I felt like I was a teenager again," says R. J., 27.

SAY THIS, NOT THAT!

SAY THIS: *How've you been?*

NOT: *Why didn't you call me before?*

BECAUSE: *He's calling now, and that's a good thing.*

SAY THIS: *I'm going to yoga tonight, but maybe we can get together after.*

NOT: *I was going to go to yoga, but I can skip it.*

BECAUSE: *Having an agenda is more appealing than being accommodating.*

SAY THIS: *What's your relationship like with your dad?*

NOT: *I want this to be a serious relationship.*

BECAUSE: *Closeness is something you earn.*

SAY THIS: *You want to start running together on Sundays?*

NOT: *I'd like to see you more often.*

BECAUSE: *Emphasize what you have in common, and he'll want to see more of you, too.*

While we do want the ultimate goal—to win the world championship of dating (with you as the trophy)—we don't want it handed to us. We want to play the game, we want to have the jitters, we want to feel some uncertainty, we want to make the plays, and we don't want to hold up the World Cup of love until we've earned it.

HOW CAN I SHOW INTEREST WITHOUT SEEMING TOO AGGRESSIVE?

My male friends complain all the time that they want women to be more aggressive, but then when a woman does get aggressive, they start referring her to as "Stalker Girl" and stuff like that. Show me the difference between *Fatal Attraction* and being too aloof.

Lots of times, men function like mobile phones in a forest—they have trouble picking up signals. But that's most likely because those signals aren't very clear. You're more verbal than we are, and often the subtlety of your words is lost on us. But while everyone knows that men are visual creatures, we're just as tactile. The key: Use your hands and your fingers. "I don't want to talk about the relationship when we first start dating, but I do like to know whether a woman thinks I'm a potential boyfriend or more like a brother," says Dane, 31. "The girl I'm dating now was really touchy when we first started, and I loved it. She wasn't overtly sexual or anything. She'd just put her hand on my shoulder, or brushed her hand down my arms, or grabbed my hips when we kissed. I could tell she just wasn't going through the motions."

Male Mysteries

19

Percentage of men who have sex on the first date *(MH)*

WONDERING WOMAN

When I ask how I look in an outfit, all he has to say is "Beautiful!" So why does he screw up the answer so often?

Probably because they've reached the weather forecast in the TV news, while he's been waiting 25 minutes for you to finish getting ready. (Nonetheless, thanks for the tip.)

HOW DO I TELL HIM I LIKE HIM WITHOUT SCARING HIM OFF?

I've gone on five dates with the guy I've been seeing. Really nice—we've laughed, had a good time, and we seem to get along great. Now we're at that awkward point—at least, awkward for me— where I want to tell him that I like him, that I'm starting to care about him. I've had bad experiences with guys where if I tell them how I feel, they end up getting really scared off and things go downhill from there. Any suggestions for the best way to tell or show a guy how much I'm into him without him freaking out and thinking that I want to marry him tomorrow?

You have to think short-term to communicate long-term. "When I first started dating my wife, it was pretty clear that we were into each other, but neither of us really talked about it," says Dylan, 39. "But what I thought was really cool was that after about a month of dating, she said she had plans to spend the weekend skiing about six weeks later and wanted to know if I wanted to join her. I jumped at it, and at the time, I didn't think much of it, but now that I look back, it seems ingenious—it was a perfect way to imply that she wanted some kind of future for our relationship without ever having to say the very annoying, 'Are we boyfriend and girlfriend?'"

WHY DO MOST MEN COME OFF AS LOSERS ON A FIRST DATE?

What's up with guys on first dates? I either get the guys who talk too much about themselves or the ones who think that the way they're going to impress me is by trying to be overly romantic and sensitive. On my last date, the guy wouldn't stop talking about his job and what he wants to do with his life, and the amazing trips he's been on. It was like he was just making sure I knew that he had money. Why does he have to try hard to make me like him?

A first date is a job interview. He knows very well that if he doesn't nail it, he doesn't get the shot at a long-term deal in what could very well be his dream situation. Unfortunately, many men overreact—thinking they have to go overboard in trying to impress the interviewer with splashy C.V.s and portfolios rather than just relaxing and letting their personality speak for itself. But the truth is, it's one of the areas where we feel really awkward. Jon, 27, says, "I hate first dates. I want her to know who I am, but if I talk too much about myself, I know it turns her off, and if I don't talk enough, then I'm afraid she's going to label me as boring." Many men go way too far in one direction or the other, but all he's trying to do is give you enough information so you'll want to call him back for a second interview.

Male Mysteries

28

Percentage of men who think it's okay to fib to get a first date

MASCULINITY MASTERED:
What You Now Know About Men

• You can win him over with light touches and lighter words.

• There's a difference between game playing and playing the game. We love the thrill, the chase, and uncertainty of finding the woman who makes us melt faster than cheese on a pizza.

• Tease. Please.

SAY THIS TONIGHT!

The sexiest thing a woman ever said to Mason, 35:

"No, do I make you comfortable?"
(In response to his question:
"Do I make you uncomfortable?")

The sexiest thing Laura, 32, ever said to a man:

"You fit me perfectly."

WHAT MEN WANT WOMEN TO KNOW ABOUT LOVE

"Love is great and men feel it as much as women, but we might be embarrassed to admit it."
—Garrett, 27

"Love is the most complicated thing to understand. Love can't be compared to beer, sex, rock and roll, or any other sacred thing to men. But when it hits, men drop like flies. Yes, we will obey!"
—Jeremy, 32

"Love doesn't make the world go 'round; it just makes the trip worthwhile."
—Alex, 39

"Love is confusing for most of us. We know if we love you or not. However, being that most of us are still 'boys,' saying 'I love you' seems kind of weird and awkward."
—Rod, 26

"This is not a soap opera."
—Brian, 25

"Even though I don't say 'I love you' after every phone conversation, it doesn't mean I don't mean it."
—Bruce, 36

"Men are more sensitive than you think. Just don't try too hard to bring that quality out in them."
—Brady, 35

"Sometimes, men talk with their subtle actions, not with their mouths."
—Chang, 34

"We like presents and backrubs, too."
—Shaun, 29

"Love is about moments."
—Tim, 34

"Love doesn't need to be talked about in order to be present."
—Dom, 38

"The quicker men say they love you, the quicker they'll fall for somebody else."
—Trent, 29

"It's okay to be naked all day."
—Michael, 24

"Men want more than sex in a relationship. We like to be loved for who we are. That old anecdote that 'men give love for sex' is just bogus. Men who claim that they only want sex are insecure and not in touch with who they are."
—Lee, 33

Chapter 15

Why Do Men Need to Be Alone?

Would you believe — because it makes us better lovers? Here's what really happens when guys are left to their own devices — and why your relationship will be all the better for it.

QUESTION: Guys, to whom do you turn for relationship advice?

Best male friend: . . . . **17 PERCENT**

Male friend: . . . . **15 PERCENT**

Female friend: . . . . **14 PERCENT**

Mother or father: . . . . **10 PERCENT**

Brother: . . . . **3 PERCENT**

OUG, 27, A GRAPHIC DESIGNER, has been seeing his girlfriend for eight months. They'll typically spend three or four nights during the week and then all weekend together. Every couple of weeks, Doug wants to go out with his group of four or five friends he's hung out with since college. "All we do is go to a bar, watch a game, and hang out, but my girlfriend is ultra-paranoid, I don't know, I guess about me flirting around and hanging out with other women, so she gives me a

hard time every time I say I'm planning a night out with my friends," he says. "And it gets really old."

What Doug's girlfriend doesn't see is that a guy hanging out with his friends is an electrical charge *for* the relationship—not against it. You may bond with your friends over lattés and the latest TV medical drama. We bond over beer and sports.

"A few years ago, a couple of my friends started talking about how cool it would be to go on a golf trip—just four of us, with golf, cigars, beer, and going out for steaks at night," says Jack, 36, a benefits manager. "It wasn't that I was unhappy in my marriage. I just wanted to spend a few days doing guy stuff. So I arranged a trip. A few of us went out to the coast, played golf, drank a little—it was a blast. But you know what? A few weeks after I got home, my wife commented to me that I was more attentive to her, and seemed happier. It wasn't like it was conscious or anything, but I guess part of it was that I appreciated she didn't harass me for wanting to take a guys' trip, and because when I was out there, I did miss her. It totally rejuvenated me."

Relationship rejuvenation doesn't have to come in the form of men-only adventures to Brazil or golf trips to Scotland (though they're fine, too). All we need is some simple get-away time—it gives us unbridled freedom to play, drink, laugh, flirt, and bust out from our regular routines. Guy time— whether it's a weekend, a night, or a few hours for a game—is our way of entrenching ourselves in the lives we had before we met you. That doesn't mean the former life is better than the current one. It just means we need to shut the stall door every once in a while.

▶ "A guy needs a little space, some time to himself, with his friends, away from his wife or significant other," says Keith, 38. "It doesn't mean he doesn't love

SAY THIS, NOT THAT!

SAY THIS: *Whatever floats your boat.*

NOT: *Why do you waste time doing that?*

BECAUSE: *Love means humoring each other's stupid obsessions.*

SAY THIS: *I'd like to do that with you sometime.*

NOT: *Can I come along?*

BECAUSE: *If he wanted you to come this time, he would have asked.*

SAY THIS: *It would mean a lot if you would come with me.*

NOT: *Do you want to come with me?*

BECAUSE: *He doesn't want to, but he will if he knows it's important.*

*you, but it's not healthy to be with you all
the time, every single day."*

► *"Women don't understand the value of solitude.
If I want to go out and drink with my buddies,
she should understand that it's healthy,"* says
Jonathan, 23.

► *"I don't think women see guy time as a chance for us
to blow off steam. They see it as their boyfriend
acting more loose, and it makes them nervous that
they're going to enjoy their time with friends so
much that they won't come back to the relationship,"* says Eddie, 34.

The surest way to get a guy to run away from a
relationship is to smother him. Logic would dictate
that the surest way to keep him in the relationship
is to give him his own room to run.

WHY WOULD A MAN RATHER GOLF THAN SPEND A MORNING IN BED WITH ME?

**What's up with golf? Why? What's the appeal? And
what the hell do you talk about for five hours?**

You know what men talk about when they're golfing?
You. Just kidding. Men talk about three things when
they're on the golf course—the best shot they ever
made, the best shot they almost made, and the best
shot they're about to make. "We need time with other
men and we're competitive and need some outlet for
that," says Seth, 30. Take Garry, 39, who plays golf
about once a month. "I go out with the same three
guys, and we'll mostly talk about golf or sports," he
says. "But if one of the guys is having a problem, he'll
bring it up, we'll make fun of him, and then we'll go
on to talking about golf. It's a safe place to talk about
our problems; golf's just a good place to unload them
and then forget about them for a little while."

**WHAT
IT MEANS
WHEN**

**. . . He tells you
he wants to take
a weekend trip
with the guys**
*Doesn't matter whether
the backdrop is golf,
fishing, or hiking, he
needs to live the
occasional reminders of
what it was like to be a
student.*

**. . . He says he'll
be home at
midnight and
comes home
around 4**
*He doesn't want you to
believe he'll enjoy
himself without you.
Inevitably, he will.*

**. . . He flies
solo, even when
he gets regular
sex**
*Men need frequent oil
changes. Some weeks
more than others. No
offense.*

WHY CAN'T I COME ALONG WHEN HE GOES OFF WITH THE GUYS?

My husband has a college reunion in a few weeks and he hinted that he wanted to go alone. I know his college friends and they're all good guys and in steady relationships or married, so I don't think they're going to do anything totally stupid, but it almost has this bachelor-party feel to it, given the fact that I was sort of uninvited to the festivities. He's always been great about including me in everything, so this seems really odd. Should I be worried about what he's going to do? I don't want him to do something that could really ruin our relationship.

For a lot of guys, college was the oasis in the desert of boredom — it was the time when they found beer, they found women, and they found that they could play football at 3 a.m., wake up at noon, and generally avoid "real life". Good times. Your husband isn't as much excluding you as he is trying to reclaim a sip of the water. "Men need to be men, do man things, be around other men," says Rusty, 30. "Just because we don't want to do everything with you doesn't mean that we don't want to be with you. There is a part of us you can't fill."

Male Mysteries

64

Percentage of men who are happy to have time to themselves when their wives or girlfriends have plans

WHAT EXACTLY DOES HE DO WHEN HE'S OUT WITH FRIENDS?

Okay, so this is weird. My boyfriend and I have this deal where every two weeks, we have girls' and guys' night out — him with his friends, me with mine. A couple weeks back, my group just happened to end up at the same bar that they did, and when we walked in, their group of five guys was talking to two or three really good-looking girls. When I approached, my boyfriend was cool — it wasn't like he was trying to hide anything. But the whole scene made me uncomfortable about what was happening. If this is the way "guys' night" is going to be, that's not really what I thought it was. I was under the impression it was beer and watching sports. I didn't know it was on-the-prowl night. I'm not sure I'm on board if this is the way it's going to be.

Rodney, 34, has been married for five years and his best friend has been married for 12 years. Once a month, they grab dinner, then drinks. "We usually go out to the real hopping places. Everybody's about five or six years younger, but it's no big deal," he says. "I'm not really comfortable talking to strangers, but my friend is really good about making small talk, getting women to hang out with us, and just having a good time. Nothing happens; we just have fun." In big groups of men, it's only natural that they'll meet up with—and talk to—some women. In this setting, some guys are the masterminds, some guys are the accomplices, some guys are just there to watch what happens, and some guys want nothing to do with what relationship crimes may take place. But remember this: Just because he goes out with his friends doesn't mean he's out to cheat; who he is always outweighs who he's with.

Male Mysteries

50

Percentage of men who say visiting a strip club is cheating (MH)

MASCULINITY MASTERED: What You Now Know About Men

• We get more out of our interactions with our friends than just high-fives, sports chatter, and obligatory double-takes when beautiful women walk by. Guy time gives us a few moments to be out of our relationships—and that makes us better in them.

• Trying to beat the crap out of our friends in golf, basketball, pool, darts, gambling, or any other competition fills a need that we'd never be able to fill with you.

• Life was good at 21. Not better, but good. Sometimes, men like to be 21, even if they're 41.

SAY THIS TONIGHT!

The sexiest thing a woman ever said to Carlos, 28:

"Again."

The sexiest thing Kristin, 31, ever said to a man:

"Why don't you go lie down on your bed and let me have my way with you."

What Does He Really Think about Your Body?

The man in your life would never tell you this to your face. But the 2,500 men in this book aren't so ashamed. . . .

QUESTION: Guys, how often do you fantasize about another woman while you're in a relationship?

Daily: . . . . 13 PERCENT

Weekly: . . . . 10 PERCENT

Monthly: . . . . 4 PERCENT

Once in a while: . . . . 54 PERCENT

Never: . . . . 21 PERCENT

TWO YEARS AGO, PATRICK, 32, A POLICE officer, was getting ready for a night out with his wife, Lori. Lori was getting dressed, and made some comment about how she was disgusted that her trousers didn't fit the way they used to. "Then she just want into this long rant about how she can't believe she's gained 10 kilos since we were married, how frustrated she is that she can't lose weight, and started referring to herself as a fat wife," Patrick says. "What am I supposed to say? There was no way I was going to let her know that her weight bothered me."

So Patrick responded the way he's supposed to—with a steady stream of answers that reassured her that such superficial judgments had no place in their marriage. "Of course, I'd rather her be the weight she was when we were married, but I told her I loved her, I still found her sexy, that I didn't care about it, which is all pretty much true, but maybe just sugar-coated a little," he says.

Truth is, we do care.

"Don't believe it when a man says he doesn't care about looks, or about the weight you gained," says Trent, 35. "Some men try to be nice and don't want to hurt a woman's feelings, but we all do put a high value on a sexy body. Every guy notices a sexy body and values it a lot."

But maybe we don't care as much as you think—or for the reasons why you may think. Let's look at the facts: one-third of men say they're secretly critiquing their partner's body while they're having sex, and a third say they're not satisfied with their partner's current weight. But there's more to the story than some guys holding women to unfair standards of being curvy in some areas and flat in others. We care about your body because better bodies simply get us more excited. (How's that for a simple truth about testosterone?) There's another reason, too— and it has more to do with what you do with your body than what we do with it. The better you feel about your body, the more you'll do with ours.

► *"My wife had been dieting and when she finally reached her target weight she lost a lot of her inhibitions about her body. The*

SAY THIS, NOT THAT!

SAY THIS: *How do I look?*

NOT: *Do you think I look fat?*

BECAUSE: *He won't think it until you mention it.*

SAY THIS: *You're sexy.*

NOT: *Do you still find me sexy?*

BECAUSE: *The best way to get the compliments you want is to give them.*

SAY THIS: *Having sex in the dark makes me feel like an animal.*

NOT: *Don't turn on the lights! I don't want you to see my cellulite.*

BECAUSE: *Calling attention to your body image problems won't make you or him feel any randier.*

day she met her goal, she was waiting for me wearing a little black dress and candles were all over the house and we had the greatest sex when I walked in the door," says Robert, 39.

► *"My wife is great at sex. She has a great body and she enjoys sex. My ex-wife also had a great body, but she wasn't confident about it, and didn't 'do much' during sex. I don't think she enjoyed it, so we didn't do it very often,"* says Jim, 43.

► *"The best was with a woman I met on a bike tour. She was as fit as I was and wonderful to touch. She had the tightest body of any woman I've ever been with,"* says Joel, 23.

Do we like your body for our own self-indulgent reasons? Of course. But we also care about how you use it just as much as whether you want to flaunt it. Fact is, we get more physical pleasure—indirectly and directly—when your body is at its best, and, more important, when the way you think about your body is even better.

WHY DO MEN WANT THE LIGHTS ON?

I'm shy in bed. Sorry. I know my husband is probably frustrated, but I just don't like lights, and I don't like being naked. It's not that my body is all that bad, except for the fact that my butt is bigger than I like it. Why does he have to look?

"Men really are turned on by how you look. That's how you get the engine revving," says Harry, 29. But don't mistake our love, our appreciation, and our lust for your body as a message that our eyes are the primary vehicles through which we derive pleasure. No lights? Fine. Want to wear some clothes? Okay. Want me to ignore certain spots of your body because you're self-conscious about them? Say the word. When it comes to sex, your comfort will be our pleasure. "I just want my girlfriend to get on top of me, which she doesn't like to do, because I know she's self-conscious because she thinks she has a belly," says Derek, 27. "I'd much rather have her into being uninhibited and into all kinds of sex than to have the best body in the world and lie there." In other words, if you

Male Mysteries

43

Percentage of men who think that it's sexier for a woman to wear an article of clothing during sex than be completely naked (the top three being a teddy, stockings, and high-heeled shoes) *(MH)*

WHAT IT MEANS WHEN

. . . He knows the storylines on TV shows meant for teenagers
It's the acceptable (marginally, albeit) way to sneak glimpses of way-too-young-for-him hotties in bikinis.

. . . He turns the lights off for sex
It's not because he doesn't want to see your body (he does! he does!). He just feels as awkward as you with full-blast lights on. Best scenario: dimmer, soft lighting.

. . . He says he likes your haircut
He likes it longer better.

need certain things just right in order to feel comfortable, that's fine. But then go ahead and feel comfortable—and let us have it!

WHY WON'T HE HELP ME LOSE WEIGHT?

I've been upfront with my husband about the fact that I'm not happy with my body—that I'd like to lose some weight, that I'd like to get rid of my post-baby weight, that I'd like to start eating better, and all that stuff. But he's not being very supportive about it. He won't talk about it, he won't go to the gym with me (even though he could stand to lose some weight), and he's not even trying to encourage me. I'm sure he'll be happy if I can get down a couple sizes, so why isn't he being more supportive?

Because talking to you about your weight is like walking through a lion cage in a suit made of tenderloin. "When my wife went on a diet recently, I started off being encouraging and helpful, trying to tell her stuff about things I had read about nutrition and exercise," says Louis, 44. "After a while, I felt like I was more like a coach than husband, and I felt like I was being condescending. She never said it bothered her, but I was really uncomfortable talking about it."

I think your husband is hedging because he doesn't want you to think he's unhappy with your body or that he loves you any less. My guess is that it's not because he doesn't want to give you support; it's because he's afraid that what you say you want may not be what you really do want.

Male Mysteries
58
Percentage of men who say a woman's intelligence is sexier than a great body

HOW DO MEN FEEL ABOUT COSMETIC SURGERY?

I'm 39 years old and, well, things aren't quite falling the way they used to. I'm not really overweight, but I'd like to make a few little adjustments. I'd like to get a breast lift and maybe even a little lipo around my belly. I mentioned this to my husband and I thought he'd be all in favor of it, but he was nonchalant, even saying he thought it was a waste of money. I'm happy he's happy with my body, but why wouldn't he support me if he knew it made me happier about my body?

Men, as you know, can be more protective than a mama bird. While he would certainly benefit from your new nips, tucks, and adjustments, he also knows that the hundreds of men who see you every day will get some kind of benefit, too. "My wife got a few things done, and she definitely felt better about herself, but I'd say she got borderline cocky about the way she looked. She strutted, she had more attitude," says Joseph, 37, whose wife had breast implants and a tummy tuck. "The surgeries didn't just change her body. They changed her." Most men are happier to have their women look their best and feel their best; they're just squeamish about change, even when it's for the better.

MASCULINITY MASTERED: What You Now Know About Men

• Your body is all about feel: How you feel about it, and how often we can feel it.

• Few things in life give us more pleasure than seeing, touching, and intertwining with your body.

• If you want an honest opinion about your body, go to a trainer or a doctor. We may have opinions, but we're not crazy enough to share them.

SAY THIS TONIGHT!

The sexiest thing a woman ever said to Bobby, 24:

"Big boy."

The sexiest thing Suzy, 33, ever said to a man:

"All I have on is my radio."

Chapter 17

Why Do Men Work So Much?

We work so much because we're scared to death of not working. Here, the soothing words that will turn any "workaholic" into a happy homebody.

QUESTION: Guys, which one-time life boost would make you feel best?

Scoring a 50-percent raise: . . . . 35 PERCENT

Losing 20 pounds immediately: . . . . 29 PERCENT

Working less, spending more time with the family: 17 PERCENT

None of these: . . . . 11 PERCENT

Dating a celebrity/supermodel: . . . . 8 PERCENT

SOMETIMES, I KNOW, IT SEEMS THAT our job gets to ride shotgun, while you're stuck in the backseat. Our job gets all of our time, attention, and effort, while you're wondering why the hell we can't put a fraction of that same chutzpah into our relationship with you.

"My girlfriend has about had it with me," says Byron, 34, who is part of a start-up company that develops medical technology. "I've been working long hours during the week, and then I go into the office for a few hours on Saturday and I usually do some work on Sunday, too. We got into this huge fight—about how work always comes first, that it's never enough, that I never take time for her anymore. I've tried telling her that I don't really have a choice. If I tell my boss I can't handle the work or if I just don't do it, I look incompetent and won't advance or see more benefits down the line. She says she'd understand if I was getting paid overtime, but her point is that working extra isn't getting me anything extra—except more work. And she's right—it's not about money. I don't want to be just one of the workers; I want to be *the* guy."

The guy.

That basic instinct—the same one that drove us to win you over—is the same one that drives us to work so often and so hard. In fact, about one-third of men say that, besides their personality, their career is the one thing that they think defines their character to other people. We put a lot of emphasis on the fact that what we do can reveal who we are.

And that's the very reason why we work like a jackhammer. Not working so hard is not a choice; it's a personal failure, a disappointment, a chink in our character. Practically, we can handle losing a job, because we know we could find another one. What we can't handle is being (and being viewed as) mediocre.

Jeremy, 42, a vice president for a major clothing company, says his wife, who also works, told him she was tired of the fact that he worked all the time—that even when he's not working, he carries the stress he has at work back home.

"What really ticked her off was that we had planned to go away for three days, just the two of us, and the day before we left, I got socked

---

SAY THIS, NOT THAT!

SAY THIS: *Can we pick a night this week when we can meet for dinner?*

NOT: *Do you have to work late AGAIN?*

BECAUSE: *It's more helpful to ask for what you want than complain about what you're not getting.*

SAY THIS: *You work so hard, we should do something fun tonight.*

NOT: *You work too much.*

BECAUSE: *He needs your support. Without it, nothing feels like fun.*

SAY THIS: *If you lose your job, you'll find a better one.*

NOT: *If you lose your job, we'll scrape by.*

BECAUSE: *Your confidence fuels his confidence.*

with this project that I had to do for a client," he says. "It's not like I could change it around, but my wife says I should have told my boss and my client that I wasn't available and couldn't work on it until after I got home. I told her that the whole reason we can take nice trips and have a nice home and all that is because I work so much. So on this trip, I ended up working about three hours for one day of the trip and about six the next. I know it wasn't right to her, but I felt like I didn't have a choice."

Now Jeremy has a deal with his wife. They try to go on two week-long vacations and a bunch of short trips every year. Since he's in a job where he has to stay connected to what's happening at work, he's agreed that one week a year, he leaves his mobile phone turned off—no matter what. "It's not ideal, but it's better," he says.

Yes, we'd much rather be at the beach than at the keyboard. Yes, we'd like to be able to on-off our work stress the minute we get home. Yes, we'd like to slice double-digit hours off our workweek. But it's just that sometimes, our ego, our drive, and our quest for an impeccable reputation are what get in the way.

WHY CAN'T HE SCALE BACK?

My husband, no lie, is working about 80 hours a week. He works 8 to 8 every day, comes home, unwinds for an hour, and then goes to the computer for another couple of hours, plus a couple of hours on Saturday. It's not a money issue; we make enough between the two of us to do well. I know he wants to do well and get promotions and all that, but why in the world is he sacrificing time in our relationship to work so much? It's not like the work is ever going to end, so why can't he learn to put it away or to delegate or to do something to make his work life more manageable?

WHAT IT MEANS WHEN

. . . He wears a sports jersey after the age of 25
Call him what you want—nerd, poser, whatever. He may be any or all, but for many men, sports serves as the landing strip for testosterone, competition, and often, a little passion.

. . . He says he has to work late, again
More times than not, he wants to get ahead, or keep from getting behind—not necessarily that he's getting someone's behind.

. . . He goes on an organizing rampage at home
He's got professional PMS. Cleaning, organizing, decluttering helps him deal with work, deadlines, stress.

WONDERING WOMAN

Why do guys try so hard to be the funniest person at the table? It's like watching amateur night at a comedy club—painful.

Because every woman in every movie, in every reality show, in every gossip column, in every magazine article, in every bitch session, in every walk of life says the guy she wants is the one with the sense of humor.

To him, it's not a choice between you and his stack of manila folders. "My wife thinks that if I spend more time at work that I'm putting work first," says Conner, 30. "To me, it's not an either-or situation. I expect my wife to understand the pressure I have at work, and think she ought to see that I need to succeed and do well in order to make money so we can have a good life." A lot of men can't put work down—because they're afraid that when they stop, so will everything else.

SHOULD I BE WORRIED IF MY BOYFRIEND CAN'T COMMIT TO ONE JOB?

I've been seeing my boyfriend for four years, and in that time, he's had six different jobs. Granted, they're all in the same line of work, but he changes companies a lot more than I think is normal for a 33-year-old guy. This is the usual pattern: He gets a job, says he loves it for a few months, then complains about getting so unfairly treated and dumped on that he's just got to get out of it. I'm all for him making changes, but something doesn't seem right. Am I making too much of this?

I'm not his shrink, and I'm not one to judge a guy who sees opportunities to advance his career. But like you, I am skeptical. It makes me wonder who's really not happy—your boyfriend or the people he's working for. While it's true that some men are hiders and some men are climbers when it comes to work, the question you should try to answer—because this affects his relationship with you—is whether he's running to something or away from it.

Male Mysteries

8

Percentage of men who say that, after personality, money is what defines his character

WHY CAN'T HE PUT AS MUCH EFFORT INTO OUR HOME LIFE AS HE DOES HIS WORK LIFE?

The other night, my husband tried to fix a dent we have in the wall. Long story, but he patched it up—and it looks, to put it mildly, like crap. I was pretty mad that he put so little effort into it, and I told him that it's funny that he can work so hard at work and be the company star, but he's got to cut corners when it comes to doing stuff like this. He denied it, said he spent time on it, and that he just messed up. But I've seen this a lot from him. He'll take his time to be perfect at work, but not when it comes to doing stuff around the house. What's up with that?

It's because his audience at work would fill a small stadium. His audience at home is you. He assumes (obviously wrongly) that you'll accept some flaws and some imperfections because at work, no one will. "My wife has accused me of rushing through jobs at home. 'You'd never do that at work,' she'll say," says Xavier, 30. "I guess I can't deny it, but I'm not really doing it maliciously. If I'm being honest, I just don't have the energy to play a perfect game all the time at both work and home."

Male Mysteries

63

Percentage of men who say it's sexy to date a woman who makes more money than he does

MASCULINITY MASTERED: What You Now Know About Men

• We work to fill a lot of basic needs—ego stroking being one of them.

• To climb the ladder, we feel like we have to take three steps at a time. If we miss a rung, we fear that the whole thing will collapse and we'll have to start way back at the bottom.

• We feel guilty as it is that we have to work when it's supposed to be our time together. If you can wait to confront us until after our stressful stretch ends, then we can talk about finding ways to separate work and home time to make us both happy.

SAY THIS TONIGHT!

The sexiest thing a woman ever said to Cam, 30:

"I'm not wearing any underwear."

The sexiest thing Alexis, 28, ever said to a man:

"You're the man I'm psyched to make love to every day for the rest of our lives."

Chapter 18

What Does a Guy's Opening Line Really Mean?

How to tell a nice guy with a bad line from a bad guy with a nice line — and start on the right foot for once!

QUESTION: Men, what might you lie about to get a first date? (Respondents could choose more than one.)

That I'm interested in more than just sex: . . 58 PERCENT

My income: . . . . 35 PERCENT

My willingness to commit: . . . . 34 PERCENT

My marital status: . . . . 20 PERCENT

Other: . . . . 20 PERCENT

THERE. WE SEE YOU. OVER THERE. YES, WE see the harp-like way you run your fingers through your hair, we see the way your eyes laugh when your friend tells a joke, we see you in your tight V-neck that sends electrical impulses spiraling from our brains to every appendage. From the moment we notice you, we know we'd much rather be talking to you than staring at you. Only problem? The bridge from us to you is a rickety one, with no guardrails, and there's a mighty steep drop to a very public—and humiliating—crash.

And that makes the me-to-you journey the one trip we're hesitant to make. See?

▶ *"Plain and simple. We're scared of rejection, no matter how much we pretend we're not,"* says Brad, 29.

▶ *"Most men lack self-confidence when approaching beautiful women, even if sex is not on their mind right at that very moment,"* says Jeffrey, 31.

▶ *"I go out with friends to bars, but I swear, every time I decide to talk to a woman, I feel like I'm back playing Little League and somebody's throwing a pitch at me. I don't know whether the thing's going to nail me or if I'm going to swing and miss or if I may actually make contact,"* says Zach, 24.

▶ *"Sometimes, we want to be chased. The sexiest thing in the world is a girl hitting on you,"* says Craig, 30.

▶ *"Men are scared to death of rejection. I would rather suffer through being alone forever than risk being rebuffed,"* says Oliver, 34.

While there are certainly some guys who have the swagger, charisma, and confidence to talk to anyone anytime, anywhere (or at least appear to have the swagger, charisma, and confidence), there are many more of us who would rather subject ourselves to an iPod's worth of Enya than approach a female stranger (especially if she's with a group of her friends).

SAY THIS, NOT THAT!

SAY THIS: *We should go out sometime.*

NOT: *Up to anything interesting this weekend?*

BECAUSE: *Most men are too humble to assume that anything other than a direct request could be a come on.*

SAY THIS: *What kind of stuff are you into?*

NOT: *What do you do for a living?*

BECAUSE: *You're interested in his passions, not his salary.*

SAY THIS: *Should we go someplace private?*

NOT: *Silence.*

BECAUSE: *Guys are worried about coming on too fast too soon—so if you want things to go further, make that crystal clear.*

SAY THIS: *You're a great kisser.*

NOT: *Silence.*

BECAUSE: *A little encouragement will make him more confident—which translates to a better experience for you.*

That's because few other situations in our lives so powerfully pose the possibility of rejection.

Jeff, 24, who designs home-stereo systems, was at a restaurant when he ran into a woman he had met briefly through one of his friends at work. They talked for a few minutes as she was on her way out. "I don't know what it was, but something just clicked, so I decided I was going to call her," he says. "Two days later, I called her and we went out. I'm still dating her nine months later, but I never told her that it took me a full hour of pacing and planning what I was going to say before I actually dialed that first time. I know it's so juvenile, but I was as nervous as I've ever been about calling a woman—because I knew how cool she was and I didn't want to blow it."

Jeff felt like he had the green light because they (sort of) already knew each other, but the situation gets more uncomfortable than yesterday's boxers when we're dealing with total strangers. Charles, 34, who is a prosecutor, says he just doesn't have any confidence in approaching strangers. "I'm single, have a good job, am decent looking, I guess, and it's not like I'm not used to talking to people. But there's always something that holds me back from making the first move with a woman," Charles says. "I feel all stilted and planned when I try to approach them cold. I just wonder how many opportunities I've blown because I was such a wimp about making a first move."

The same question goes to you: How many opportunities have you missed because the guy was too much of a wimp to make the first move? Is that your fault? Maybe. You can help us—help us cross that about-to-break bridge—by remembering that we're as lumpy as a bachelor's mashed potatoes when it comes to our initial approach. Give us a sign—or

WHAT IT MEANS WHEN

. . . He's at a bar by himself
He's comfortable being alone at the bar, maybe not so much about being alone in life.

. . . He offers to cook you dinner for your third date
He has life skills (to show you he'd make a good mate), he has a clean place (to show you he'd make a good mate), and he has high-thread-count sheets (in case you'd like to mate).

. . . He grabs your phone and programs his number in it
He dares you to text him within 24 hours. Up for a game of relationship chess?

WONDERING WOMAN

When he looks in the mirror while we're having sex, he seems more interested in watching himself than me. Explain.

Clarification: He's not looking at himself. He's looking at what you're doing to him.

two—that makes it clear that you're putting up the guardrail, and that it's safe to come on over. (Smiles work wonders.) Even better, take action yourself and cross to our side of the bridge before we even get a chance to come to yours.

WHY WON'T HE MAKE THE FIRST MOVE?

I like this guy at work: He's smart, funny, doesn't take himself too seriously. I know he broke up with his girlfriend a few months ago. I'm single and wouldn't mind getting together with him, but I'm definitely not going to make the first move by asking him out. I feel like I've been giving him some signals—stopping by his office a little more than usual, inviting him to lunch with a few of us from my department. He seems to be interested, but he hasn't done anything about it. Can't he see I'm interested?

Some guys are just thicker than an octogenarian's glasses. No matter what their experience, guys try to read signals, but they often get all crossed up. With you, it could be that he sees your signals and is debating the pros and cons of dating a colleague, or it could be that he's already canoodling with Sarah from sales. Either way, it seems like you're being about as clear as a mirror in a steam room. Yes, we love flirting, but we also love women who strike first. "In my life, I've had only three women who were ballsy enough to ask me out," says Kyle, 30. "I have to tell you, whether I was interested in them or not, I think it's the biggest turn-on for a guy—for a woman to flirt, to talk, and to be the first one to start a conversation. Besides taking the pressure off of us, it's damn impressive when a woman has the courage to do something that we can't."

WHAT MAKES A WOMAN APPROACHABLE TO A MAN?

When I'm out, I know what I like when I see it. I look at how a man looks, how he dresses, and how he carries himself. But I'm just curious if a guy goes through the same mental checklist. What's a guy looking for when he decides to approach a woman? Besides looks, I mean. Let's just say that the place is full of hotties. How does a man decide who he's going to talk to?

It's impossible to know. At first, a guy is like a NASA computer—he immediately takes in all the data about looks and overall vibe, then processes it faster than you can order another white wine. Then he turns into a surveillance crew. He watches. And watches. And thinks. And debates. And watches. And asks his buddies what they think. And watches. Often he goes home alone because he spent so much time working up to his big moment that he missed it. No doubt, he'll have a radar-lock on you, but it will be a while before he decides to take his shot.

Male Mysteries

33

Percentage of men say it's more enjoyable to be dating than to be married

WHAT'S WITH THE CHEESY PICKUP LINES, ANYWAY?

This guy walked up to me at a bar, looked me up and down and asked me if I was hurt, because I must've fallen from heaven. Please. There's nothing—I mean *nothing*—that impresses me about a guy who uses an opening line that he got from some corny movie. Why in the world does any guy think that those kinds of lines are going to impress a woman?

I wish I could tell you, because using a pickup line is like using a plastic spoon in a knife fight. But here's the thing. A man, approaching you cold, has about seven seconds grace before you assess whether you're going to turn toward him or away from him. Many men don't feel like they have the verbal arsenal to win you over in 25 words or less, so they resort to any opening they can find. "My female friends always tell me that pickup lines are the worst, but I've talked to lots of women after using them, I think because they actually laugh at them that they're so bad," says Jerry, 23. We know the things that we're supposed to do to get your attention—ask questions, start natural conversation—but if you want us to take that approach, you have to give us one thing we don't have: A little time to give you a pickup paragraph or two.

MASCULINITY MASTERED: What You Now Know About Men

• We may exude confidence when we approach you. Truth is, our stomachs are churning faster than an out-of-balance washing machine.

• To us, you are like a star basketball player. You have the ability to block any shot we want to throw. Before you swat it back in our face, let us hoist it up there. We appreciate your giving us an open look at the basket.

• We'll wait longer than you think to make a move. Which means it's fine by us for you to do it instead.

SAY THIS TONIGHT!

The sexiest thing a woman ever said to Justin, 29:
"Thank you."

The sexiest thing Amelia, 28, ever said to a man:
"These clothes look good on you, but I'd rather see you naked."

Chapter 19

How Can I Get Him to Focus on Foreplay?

Some simple tricks for slowing him down —
and speeding you up.

QUESTION: Guys, what would you most want
to change about your sex life?

More sex: . . . . 20 PERCENT

Longer sex sessions, more foreplay: . . . . 15 PERCENT

More and/or better oral sex . . . . 9 PERCENT

More passion with partner: . . . . 6 PERCENT

YOU KNOW THE CLICHÉ: WOMEN ARE
campfires, and men are blowtorches. Women
want the fire to burn long and slow, and men
want to strike quick and fast. Men want to hit it
and quit it. In and out. Wham bam. But if you
really want us to thank you, ma'am, then know this: The male experience
of sex isn't all about the few minutes between the time he invades your
inner sanctum and the time he releases his rebels. They're also in it for

what's happening to earlobes, lips, tongues, and any other body parts you want to offer up as an appetizer.

Do we like quickies? Yes, of course, we do. We like them for the same reason we like microwave meals—because they let us satisfy our urges in about the same amount of time it would take us to, say, arm wrestle an underweight starlet. But quickies usually have a lot more going for them than just the zip and unzip aspects.

Doug, 26, a financial assistant, has been with his girlfriend for about a year. And he says his most memorable sex comes when it happens like a drag race—to see how fast he can get from 0–60. "We don't have quickies too often, but when we do, it's because we either have to be somewhere or we're trying to hide. Early on in the relationship, we had sex in the bathroom at a party—and it was so good because it was so fast and so risky."

In the case of men who want fast sex at other times, there's also something else going on: We're seeking immediate stress relief.

"There are times when I really feel like I need to have sex—just for the pure physical release, and I'm not sure my wife really understands that," says Reed, a 34-year-old small-business owner. "I work and worry about work a lot, and sex is one of those things that takes my mind off everything. I want, too, that connection with her that comes from sex, but sometimes I'm too wrapped up in everything to have those long sessions we both enjoy."

Reed isn't the only guy who likes quickies

SAY THIS, NOT THAT!

SAY THIS: *Let's slow down. I want to enjoy every single second.*

NOT: *I need more foreplay!*

BECAUSE: *Barking orders in bed isn't sexy—unless you're both into S&M.*

SAY THIS: *Tell me when you start getting close.*

NOT: *Don't come yet!*

BECAUSE: *It'll already be too late.*

SAY THIS: *Oooh, what you were just doing felt so amazing. Can you do that again?*

NOT: *Silence.*

BECAUSE: *Telling him exactly what's working will boost his ego and get you the sex you want.*

SAY THIS: *This handy little device is going to prevent you from getting arthritis when you're 80.*

NOT: *Can we use my vibrator? It works much better.*

BECAUSE: *He'll be game as long as he doesn't feel inferior.*

but also craves long, languid lovemaking. A full 31 percent of men say their foreplay sessions aren't long enough, and if you look at how some guys in our poll describe their best sexual experiences, there's a common theme: lots of buildup, lots of anticipation, lots of foreplay, lots of pregame warmups, lots of great sex that was great because of what happened *before* the actual sex. Sound familiar?

► *"The best sex we had was coming home from the bar after a night of listening to live music, drinking, and hanging out with friends,"* says Gregory, 23. *"The whole night was spent having fun and it just led to an amazing experience when we got home, too."*

► *"My best sex: We frequently paused and prolonged the sex and mixed in more foreplay,"* says Alan, 32. *"In the end, it was better than anything I've ever felt."*

► *"I was on a business trip with an associate, who I had been flirting with for a couple of months,"* says Peter, 37. *"We got along great, but never really acted on it. On this trip, we couldn't stop touching each other throughout the day. After dinner, we ended up in her room watching a movie with a bottle of wine. One thing led to another and the next morning, there she was, naked and cuddled right next to me."*

I think a lot more men are into foreplay than you realize:

► *"Foreplay is great. If you'd do more of it, so would we,"* says Lyle, 36.

► *"We like to be attended to every once in a while. Not simply oral sex, but in other, more sensual ways, too,"* says Carlton, 34.

► *"Men love foreplay—especially when the woman acts as if she's really into him,"* says Keith, 34.

WHAT IT MEANS WHEN

. . . He does what he can to give you an orgasm before he has one

Though he enjoys pleasuring you, sexual patience for men is a biological struggle. His body is telling him to go, but his brain convinces him he'll be handsomely rewarded if he yields.

. . . He asks if he can give you a massage

It's a lot smoother than asking you to remove your shirt.

. . . He kisses your neck

He strongly endorses nudity within the next few minutes.

Why does he think having sex to a blasting rock band like AC/DC is romantic?

His fantasy isn't always to have sex on the beach, with Luther Vandross ballads kissing your collective ears. Sometimes, his fantasy is a little more staccato. SHORT SKIRTS. DRUNK NIGHTS. POUND POUND. UP AGAINST THE WALL. SLICK SWEAT. OPEN MOUTHS. YEAH BABY. ROCK ON.

Women sometimes don't realise that for men, the anticipation of having sex can be just as nerve jostling and whoa-ho-ho-inducing as the climactic moment. You may think that all men care about is how much attention is paid to the goal post, when in reality, we want you to play with our entire field—and we really want to spend some time doing the same for you.

WHY CAN'T I BE AFFECTIONATE WITHOUT HIM THINKING I WANT SEX?

Whenever I kiss or hug or show any affection for my boyfriend, he thinks it's an invitation to have sex. I feel like I can't even offer to give him a massage because I think he'll automatically assume we'll be having sex after that. Why does he expect to have sex every time I show a physical sign of affection?

I'm not sure that he *expects* to have sex as much as he *wants* to have sex. You take physical contact as a sign of affection, but with us, any kind of physical contact between consenting adults is like the bugler at the start of a horse race. It's the signal that something's about to begin, and we're in the starting gate ready to run. "My wife once complained that she can't even give me a hug without me doing something or saying something dirty," says Fred, 40, who's been married for six years. "But honestly, and I know this going to sound weird, I get excited when we touch each other—even if it's meant to be innocent." Maybe men need to be more sensitive to the fact that every butt-pat and hug isn't meant to be a green light to the Barry White CD, but the fact is that our engine is always idling, and if you put us into gear, our instinct is to press the accelerator pedal and see how far we can get.

WHAT CAN I DO TO GET HIM OUT OF A SEXUAL RUT?

Every time my husband and I have sex, it starts out the same way. We both undress ourselves, and then he kisses me for a minute or two. Then he's onto my breasts, touches me a little bit in the hot spot, and then expects me to be ready for sex. It's not that it's bad, but I just wish he'd pay attention to all of my body. Why is it so hard for him to mix things up a little and take his time?

For one, he's stimulating himself as much as he is trying to stimulate you (news alert: *he's* turned on when he touches your breasts). The other reason is that both of you are in a sexual holding pattern. You have sex at the same times of the week, the same times of day, and the same way. So it shouldn't be a surprise that he follows the same connect-the-dots pattern during foreplay. Yes, he needs to take responsibility for mixing it up, but you can also take the baton and lead this orchestra. "The best sex I have with my wife comes out of nowhere," says Lawrence, 27, who's been married for two years. "One time, we were at the mall, she kissed me and then whispered a simple 'I'm really horny' into my ear, so we dropped everything to get out of there. Foreplay started in the car, and we ended up in a naked, sweaty pile at home."

Male Mysteries

50
Percentage of men who say they're better in bed than their wives or girlfriends

24
Percentage of men who refused to answer that question

IF A GUY IS GETTING REGULAR SEX, WHY DOES HE STILL MASTURBATE?

My boyfriend, who lives with me, needs to get up about a half-hour before I do to go to work. The other morning, he was in the shower, and I got up to use the bathroom and I saw him taking care of his own business. I know that guys do that, but I figured that since we have sex three or four times a week (including the night before!), there'd really be no need for him to do it. It made me wonder how often he does it, and why I haven't been able to satisfy him. What makes a guy want to go at it by himself, especially when he's in a relationship that includes a lot of sex?

Trevor, a 32-year-old electrical engineer, says he has a good sex life; he has sex twice a week and he has no complaints. "My wife's great, but I just need to take care of things myself sometimes," Trevor says. "Like when I can't fall asleep, I'll do it quietly, and it helps me go to sleep. I think women think masturbation is some kind of ultra-sexual thing, like doing it means we're not attracted to the woman we're with. For me at least, it's more about stress relief than sexual satisfaction." Truth is, your boyfriend is completely satisfied with you (especially if you're having sex three or four times a week!). There are just those times when he craves a quickie for whatever reason, so he finds the shortest path to that result. And having a healthy sex life means he's sexually revved up—in fact, the more you have sex, the more he's primed for sex, and the more he may need to relieve himself. Even though there are lots of things that can inspire him to buff lil' Elvis's blue suede shoe (memories, fantasies, your copy of *Cosmo*), he'd much rather have you involved. On the satisfaction meter, doing it by ourselves may outrank not doing it all. But it *never* outranks doing it with you.

MASCULINITY MASTERED:
What You Now Know About Men

• We can do it in 30 seconds, but we'd usually prefer it over 30 minutes.

• Everyone knows that the pre-final hype is almost always better than the actual game. When it comes to sex, the hype, the anticipation, and the hope of something good to come is the second reason why we love foreplay just as much as the big game. (The first, of course, is your breasts.)

• Sex serves many purposes, including both bonding with you and releasing our pent-up stress.

SAY THIS TONIGHT!
The sexiest thing a woman ever said to Jake, 36:
"You're the best I've ever had."

The sexiest thing Daniela, 22, ever said to a man:
"Want to see my tattoo?"

WHAT MEN WANT WOMEN TO KNOW ABOUT SEX

"Sex is a powerful catalyst for a relationship."   —Nicholas, 27

"Sex is the reward for love."   —Benjamin, 34

"A man's sexual appetite is much like his . . . appetite. An orgasm for a man is like three trips to the buffet line. Most men just want to close their eyes and take a nap. A few men are polite enough to pretend to still want to go someplace and have dessert. I guess it's men's equivalent of faking an orgasm."   —Dave, 30

"All men aren't craving sex every waking moment any more than women are."   —Andrew, 24

"For men, sex is like an oil change. We get downright cranky if we don't get it regularly."   —Aidan, 23

"Don't just do it to do it. If you're going to have a real relationship with someone, the sex has to bring both of you closer together."   —Karl, 31

"A man secretly wants their partner to be pleased. A man's own pleasure is icing on the cake."   —Lars, 37

"Sex without love is fun, but sex with love is better."   —Billy, 25

"Put your back into it."   —Bob, 30

"Enjoy your sexuality and femininity and show it. Surprise him with a candid picture of yourself and put it in his wallet. E-mail him what you're wearing, or not wearing. Tell him what turns you on."   —Vincent, 28

"Sex can be emotional, physical, or spiritual, but not necessarily at the same time and place."   —Marc, 38

"Foreplay is what excites men."   —Les, 42

"Variety is good, intensity is good, enthusiasm is better."—Jesse, 23

"Use teeth with permission."   —Brad, 26

"Take off your shell, and your rules, with your clothes."   —Chuck, 30

Chapter 20

What Really Scares a Man?

Not being a god to our wife and kids.
Here's how to help him master his fear
of failure and make him commit to you.

QUESTION: Men, what was your father's primary role when you
were growing up, and what is your role as a parent today?

Percentage who say their father's parenting role was the breadwinner: 49.7

Percentage who say their father's parenting role was the disciplinarian: 24

Percentage who say their father's parenting role was a teacher: 15

Percentage who say their father's parenting role was a friend: 11

Percentage who say his parenting role is the breadwinner: 20

Percentage who say his parenting role is the disciplinarian: 7

Percentage who say his parenting role is a teacher: 42

Percentage who say his parenting role is a friend: 32

GRANTED, WE CAN NEVER KNOW
what it's like to become pregnant and to
physically bring a new generation into
the world. And we know, partly because
of that, mothers are the familial kings.
You'll get no argument from me: A mother's job trumps all others.

Maybe that's the reason some of us struggle so much as fathers—we're constantly seen as the backup on the parenthood team. Sure, we can coach football, build trikes, and carry three kids and a beach bag (all in one arm). But when it comes to the important stuff—the talks and the intangibles—mothers live on stage, while we sometimes toil in the orchestra pit. And we don't always like the view.

Alexander, 39, a dentist, got divorced when his son was eight. Now, he finds himself constantly trying to jockey for respect in the relationship. "I have no idea what my ex-wife says to my son about me, but I know she's not saying that I'm a good father and that I can teach him all kinds of things, so every time we get together, I'm constantly trying to reassert my position as a father, rather than just having my son know me for who I am, and it's frustrating."

Whether we're divorced or not isn't the issue. The issue is that dads are constantly battling the goofy dad syndrome that's continually seen on commercials and television sitcoms. We can take being the punchline to every inept father joke, but really, not performing as the perfect parent bothers us more than we're willing to let on.

"My four-year-old boy really loves for me to draw things so we can color them in, like a football player, or an animal, something easy," says Christian, 32, a mechanical engineer. "One time, he asked me to draw a raccoon, so I tried and it ended up looking like some kind of blob. It was horrible, and my son told me I was a terrible drawer and that his

SAY THIS, NOT THAT!

SAY THIS: *Let's decide what the rules are together.*

NOT: *I need you to enforce my rules.*

BECAUSE: *If you give him dual power as a parent, he'll take dual responsibility.*

SAY THIS: *We have to find a way to bring in more income.*

NOT: *It's about time you asked for a raise.*

BECAUSE: *The days of the de facto male provider are over.*

SAY THIS: *Your dad can teach you a lot.*

NOT: *Your father thinks he knows everything.*

BECAUSE: *If you want your kids to show respect, lead by example.*

SAY THIS: *What does offside mean?*

NOT: *Sports are a waste of time.*

BECAUSE: *It's never too late to become a fan.*

uncle could do a much better job with it. It's no big deal in the grand scheme, but it was the first time he ever said that I had done something wrong. And I have to tell you, when he compared me to my brother, it was a little punch in the gut."

Male Mysteries

54

Percentage of men who say family is what defines them the most

And that happens every time a child questions us, challenges us, spits out a "you're stupid," or makes us feel like we're 12 feet short of average when it comes to fulfilling our duties as a dad.

HOW CAN I GET MY HUSBAND TO STOP SPOILING THE KIDS?

The biggest fight that I have with my husband is how we discipline our kids. I'm always the one who disciplines the kids, stays all over them about having good manners, cleaning up, anything that has to do with their conduct. And I'll turn around and my husband is a huge softie—telling my kids yes on things I'd never say yes to (like having dessert 20 minutes before dinner). I've told him many times that this really bothers me—that he needs to be more of a disciplinarian, that he needs to be less of a friend and more of a parent. But nothing seems to get through. I'm getting really frustrated that our kids are getting mixed messages. Why does he do this?

I think he feels like he's running second to your first in a car race. When women take the lead in discipline, the guy feels like he's drafting behind—not really making decisions, just watching from back there. Sometimes, he may intentionally initiate a crash, because he feels like there's no way for him to push through and take the lead. "My wife and I

WHAT IT MEANS WHEN

. . . He coaches his kid's sports team
Don't tell him he's trying to live his glory days through his kid. He's just trying to make some glory days with his kid.

. . . He flicks through all the TV channels 12 times in a row
Men are explorers— whether it's in travel, in bars talking to women, or on bodies in bed. With TV, it's no different. He's searching for something that may give him more satisfaction than if he were to stay in one place.

. . . He has small feet
He better be a good dancer.

Is it really that hard to aim for the toilet when he takes a whiz?

Male physiology: The "whiz" stream does not travel at the same speed during the entire duration of the flow. It starts slow, accelerates to maximum speed, then decelerates as the bladder empties, eventually trickling and dripping at the end. The on-the-floor errors typically occur through speed misjudgments at the opening or ending seconds, no matter how well he holds or aims. It's not like he has a penile computer chip with radar-lock. The only 100-percent solution? Install a urinal.

sometimes fight about how we punish our kids— she tends to want to do really extreme, long-term punishments like no Xbox for a week, and I tend to suggest more short-term punishments, like sending them to their rooms for an hour," says Matthew, 32. "But I found that when I have the kids by myself, I'm a lot tougher on them. It's almost like the hard part isn't disciplining; it's negotiating the discipline with my wife."

DO MEN TRY TO BUY THEIR CHILDREN'S LOVE?

My ex-husband and I split up about three years ago when my daughter was two and my son was three. Lately, I've been seeing that my ex has been spending a little bit more money on the kids than he used to. He's spoiling them a bit, and I just think it's a little sleazy, like he's trying to buy their love. I'm starting to get pretty upset about it but I don't want to get into that terrible war that has the children picking sides. I don't even think it's malicious on his part—just his way of trying to make sure the kids love him. What should I say to him?

Not saying it's right, not saying it's entirely the same, not saying I endorse it. But you wouldn't mind receiving the same thing from a man, right? Unexpected gifts at unexpected times to reassure you that we love you? He may very well be trying to buy the same affection that you get automatically, which will never work in the long run, but remember that you have the one thing he craves more than anything else: More time with his kids.

DO ALL MEN PUT PRESSURE ON THEIR SONS?

My husband is one of those sports nuts. He's not pushing our son to go into sports per se. He tells me all the time that our son can do whatever he wants. But he's always asking my son, who's eight, if he wants to have a catch or shoot baskets, or go out and do something like that. I'm really happy my husband's involved, but I don't think he should get all the say in what our son does just because he's the man. How can I tell him that I think he's indirectly putting pressure on our son to perform?

There are three kinds of sports dads—there are the crazy coaches, who bully their kids to excel. There are the Jacques Cousteaus, who'd prefer their kids explore nature and science rather than throw knuckleballs and screen passes. And then there's a whole group of dads who want to be somewhere in the middle. This third type of dad wants to teach, he wants his kids to do well, he wants to be looked up to as the man who taught his son the mechanics of the perfect tackle, and he wants to be the one who's thanked by his kid in a *Sports Illustrated* article 15 years from now. "I remember the first time my son scored a goal in a game with other kids," says Darren, 40. "He was six, and he shot it, and it was perfect. He pumped his fist, he was so proud, and he looked over to me because he wanted to see my reaction. I don't know if he'll play much as he gets older, but I can tell you that I'll never forget the look that he gave me."

MASCULINITY MASTERED: What You Now Know About Men

• Sometimes we go against what you tell the kids even if we know we shouldn't because we want more of a say in how our kids are being raised.

• Teaching our kids about sports is only partially about sports.

• You play a huge role in what our kids think about us. We don't want to sound like a political candidate, but would you please help us, support us, endorse us?

SAY THIS TONIGHT!

The sexiest thing a woman ever said to D. W., 32:
"I . . . I . . . Oh . . . Wow."

The sexiest thing Tonya, 24, ever said to a man:
"Let's play X-rated Simon Says. You be Simon."

Chapter 21

How Do We Know If It's Over?

Why men panic and start to bail—and how to know if you should hold tight or cut the line.

QUESTION: Guys, what does your wife or girlfriend complain about most? (Respondents could choose more than one.)

My attentiveness to her needs: . . . . 28 PERCENT

My listening skills: . . . . 21 PERCENT

Foreplay/sex: . . . . 20 PERCENT

My chores around the house: . . . . 18 PERCENT

How much I work: . . . . 17 PERCENT

My driving skills: . . . . 14 PERCENT

Flirting with other women: . . . . 12 PERCENT

My ability to manage finances: . . . . 10 PERCENT

My parenting skills: . . . . 8 PERCENT

My home repair skills: . . . . 6 PERCENT

'M JUST NOT READY FOR A LONG-TERM RELATIONSHIP.
*I've been too hurt by past women. I'm too committed to my career.
I just need to get my head straight. It's not you. It's me.*

Heard that before? Let me set the record straight.

Actually, it is you.

More times than you think.

Of the men who say, "It's not you, it's me," one-third of them are lying.

Fiends! Why do we men use that line as our escape hatch? For the same reasons you've probably said it to a man. Deep down, we know the relationship won't work long-term, and it's the easiest, most painless way out. The line is a relationship getaway car—the excuse that's always standing by at the ready in case we need to get out of a sticky situation fast. Without much argument, without any opening for you to dissect what's wrong and vow to change it, without making you feel like you've been slammed, squashed, and slapped. And that's the real reason why the line works so well during a breakup: Because it cuts the head off a relationship quickly without leaving anyone squirming and writhing on the floor.

"I had one girlfriend who broke up with me and went on a tirade. She called me selfish, she said I didn't care about her, and she was basically saying I was scum when it came to being a boyfriend. I didn't think it was true, but damn if it still doesn't sting like hell when you hear it," says Daniel, 34, an outdoors photographer. "Unless something happens that's really painful, like she cheats on me, why would I want to criticize a woman when I break up with her? I don't know if this will make sense, but even after we end it, I still want her to like me, even if she hates me."

Women are far more likely to be straightforward with their complaints (see the above poll for evidence of that). Men? Well, no matter what fatal flaw we see in a woman, we'd rather just not have the conversation.

The implication of the "us, not you" line, therefore, is clear. He's lying. Really, if he wanted a future with you or if you jazzed his soul more than Coltrane, then it wouldn't matter what happened with past girlfriends,

SAY THIS, NOT THAT!

SAY THIS: *Here's what I need to be happy.*

NOT: *I'm miserable.*

BECAUSE: *Unless we can see a way to fix it, we'll assume it's broken.*

SAY THIS: *If you don't want to take the next step with me, I need to know.*

NOT: *We either take the next step or it's over.*

BECAUSE: *Demanding a decision works better than delivering an ultimatum.*

**Male
Mysteries**

24

Percentage of
men who might
accept a
one-time cash
payment from
their spouse
to end the mar-
riage

careers, or anything else. We'd drop all of our excuses, and we'd do anything to make it work.

Tommy, a 30-year-old retail manager, was in a relationship for three years when he went through a messy breakup—lots of arguing, fighting over whose stuff was whose. His girlfriend had broken up with him, and he spent some time thinking he was going to lay low, do some casual dating, and not let himself get into anything else. "About three weeks after my long relationship ended, I met a woman through a friend, and we just clicked," he says. "I wasn't ready for a long-term deal, but she just wowed me. And I ended up marrying her." It was a perfect time for the "it's not you" excuse, but as in most cases, it *was* her—and he couldn't do without her.

The way men see it, any breakup is hard—no matter who's on the giving end or receiving end. And a gentle line that maintains respect is like a boxing glove on a fist. If you're not ready for the punch, it's still going to hurt, but hopefully it helps soften the blow.

WHY DO GUYS SEEM TO BREAK UP WITH WOMEN OUT OF NOWHERE?

I went out with a guy for two years. We had been having problems. We were working in different cities, and not seeing each other that often. When I brought up the fact that things weren't going as well as they used to, he said something to the effect that he just didn't see a future for us together, that he cared for me, but didn't think he was ready for the next step. He had to have been thinking about this—or known this—for a long time. Why couldn't he have spared us both some time and pain and told me a year before?

**WHAT
IT MEANS
WHEN**

. . . He says he's not ready for a commitment
You're not the one. If you were, he'd be ready for a commitment, even if he wasn't.

. . . His best friend is a woman
Elevated threat level. Not necessarily because he wants to share a bed with her, but because he's more likely to be sharing other stuff with her—stuff about you.

WONDERING WOMAN

He tells me about his bowel movements, ingrown armpit hairs, and yellow toenails in vivid detail, but if I mention having a yeast infection, he screams ewwww! and doesn't touch me for a month. Why isn't he more comfortable talking about all aspects of my body?

You have armpits, toenails, and bowel movements, so he assumes— even though you may not admit it—that you can identify with what he's talking about. The only thing he knows about yeast has to do with beer.

I'd like to say that maybe the reason is that he's tired of being the initiator when it comes to the relationship (initiating the first date, initiating the sex). But the real reason is that even when guys are bad guys, they never want to be the bad guy—which is why we have a hard time articulating anything that could be construed as a breakup line. He doesn't want to be seen as the prick, the cheater, the lout, or the insensitive bastard who ruined the relationship, so it's easier for him to volley back rather than serving. "You know how it is when you leave a job? You always want to leave so that your old job wishes you hadn't left?" says George, 34. "You want to feel like you're still wanted. It's the same thing with women. It's not really about not burning any bridges so you can come back if you want. You just want that when she remembers you—and talks about you with all her friends—that you're in good status." Ultimately, while he may not want the relationship, he still craves a legacy.

IF HE'S NOT READY FOR A RELATIONSHIP, WHY IS HE DATING ME?

I've been seeing this guy for a couple weeks. He's cool, we enjoy each other, have a lot in common, and have slept together a couple of times. So we're on something like our sixth date, and he lays it all on me—that he's coming off a tough breakup, that he's not sure he's ready to go on, that I'm great but his head is in a messed-up place. I wasn't going to argue with the guy, but I'm tired of the B.S. Why does he use his head as an excuse for not wanting to continue a relationship with me?

Okay, let's say he's gone to this great new restaurant—a place that's hip, cool, getting lots of good attention. First time there, he tries something, likes it, goes back again, and isn't quite as impressed. So he tries something else on the menu, and then something else, and then he realizes that hey, maybe the restaurant just isn't for him. The reason why he's using his head as an excuse—and not the fact that he's not finding you to be a match—is because he thinks you're cool, smart, and attractive, but maybe just not serving the right dishes for his taste. It doesn't mean other people won't enjoy the place, and it doesn't mean it's not worthy of being open. It just means it's not for him, so you shouldn't worry about trying to keep him as a regular.

Male Mysteries

21

Percentage of men who are on the lookout for something better while they're in a relationship

WHY DO GUYS BOLT ONCE THE RELATIONSHIP STARTS TO HEAT UP?

I was going out with a guy for about a month and things started to get serious—we'd see each other several times a week, and you could just tell it was at that point where we probably would be talking about what the relationship was. I thought everything was going well, but he just out of the blue told me he wasn't ready for a serious thing. What's with the cold feet?

Because we're afraid of being tied down—even if you're not showing us your roping tricks. "A woman who's so anxious to 'lock me in' as her boyfriend doesn't realize how much of a turn-off that is. What she's basically saying to me is that she's ruling the relationship," says Laurence, 27. It's the same

HE SAID . . .

Of the married men who would accept a one-time cash payment from their spouse to end the marriage, what it would cost

Nothing:	12 percent
Just moving expenses:	22 percent
$10,000:	15 percent
$100,000:	18 percent
$1,000,000:	33 percent

principle later in the relationship, too, when we've decided we want to commit to you. The difference is that now the pressure isn't about committing; it's about performing. Not in bed, but in life. Pressure to be a good father, husband, son-in-law, trash-taker-outer, car-maintainer, money manager, roofer-negotiator, computer-fixer, DVD-programmer, and everything else. It's not that we mind doing all those things; it's that we mind doing them under your watchful eye, while fearing failure. "It doesn't matter what I do," says Brandon, 45. "I could be shoveling snow. I could be changing the oil in my car. I could be paying bills online. My wife always seems to have a better way to do things. I know she's trying to help by offering suggestions, but she doesn't even realize how nagging it is to have your every move questioned."

MASCULINITY MASTERED:
What You Now Know About Men

• When we break up with you, it's because we don't like you *that* much anymore, but we find no need to be that blunt.

• Good guys aren't the only ones who want to be remembered as such.

• If we meet the right woman, it doesn't matter how screwed up our head is; we'll find a way to screw it back on the right way. In a hurry.

SAY THIS TONIGHT!

The sexiest thing a woman ever said to Brett, 33:
"You need to teach that to other men."

The sexiest thing Ashley, 26, ever said to a man:
"How bad do you want it?"

Chapter 22

Why Won't He Tell Me about His Day?

Why are men so grumpy when they come home?
It's simple—it just takes us longer to figure out
how we're feeling. A quick course on helping your
guy access his inner self.

QUESTION: Guys, describe your average workday:

Non-stop stress, 24-7, I even go to sleep thinking about work: 9 PERCENT

Tough, but after I wind down a little bit at home, I'm okay: 20 PERCENT

Tense but I'm calm by the time I'm home: . . . . 53 PERCENT

Pretty laid back, and usually I'm ready to have fun at home: 18 PERCENT

ANT A PEEK INTO WHAT
really happens in the male
brain at about 6:45 every
weeknight? *Hi, honey, I'm
home. Yes, work was fine.*
*Now, what I'd really like to do is to get out of these trousers and change
into shorts, and go sit on the toilet and read the paper (because I didn't
have time to do either today), and then when I'm done, why yes, I'd love a
bowl of the chili you just made. In front of the TV. Because my favorite TV*

show is about to come on. Meet me back in the living room in an hour so we can catch up.

We know you want us to talk about the previous 12 hours, and yes, dear, we did miss you while we were away. But work, as you very well know from your own experience, is a bombardment of e-mail, papers, complaints, orders, whining, pressure, deadlines, and has more foul-smelling crap than a zoo. We just deal with it differently than you do. What happens in our office stays in our office for a reason. "Sometimes we just don't want to talk about problems," says Trey, 34, a computer consultant. "That's not how we relieve stress. Sometimes we just need to do something to get our mind off of problems." For instance, this is what men say they want to do as soon as they come home from work:

- ►*14 percent of men want to flip on the TV*

- ►*14 percent of men want to check e-mail*

- ►*12 percent of men want to eat*

- ►*10 percent of men want to go to the bathroom*

- ►*9 percent of men want to play with the kids*

- ►*5 percent of men want to go to the gym*

Only one in ten want to talk—meaning that 90 percent of us want to do anything but. "My wife used to work, but when we had kids, she decided to stay home," says Jake, 36, a financial analyst. "When I get home, she asks me about what happened at work. If I say 'nothing,' or don't give her many details, she gets frustrated. I tell her that the last thing I want to talk about after work is work. But she said that since she's with the kids all day, she wants to know what's happening in the real world. And to tell you the truth, most of the time,

SAY THIS, NOT THAT!

SAY THIS: *I'm so glad to finally be home!*

NOT: *Work was awful and I've been in a bad mood all day.*

BECAUSE: *Like you, he wants reassurance that you're happy to see him.*

SAY THIS: *Let's have nachos and watch something on TV.*

NOT: *You seem stressed. What happened today?*

BECAUSE: *After a bad day, food and relaxation are what he really craves, not conversation.*

SAY THIS: *Your boss is a prick.*

NOT: *Your boss has a point.*

BECAUSE: *He needs you in his corner.*

after working all day, I'm just not up for that. I want to play with the kids, shoot a few baskets in the driveway, and have dinner."

The reason? We need time to unwind, to decompress, to not think about figures, facts, and in-fighting. Aaron, 29, a project manager, says, "In one job, I had a one-hour commute, and when I got home, my girlfriend was ready to go out, have dinner, talk. But I just wanted to flop for 20 minutes. She said I had unwind time in the car. I explained to her that commuting isn't unwinding time—because I'm still thinking about that day, and all I have to do tomorrow. I just need time to chill."

Give us that time to chill. If we can stop thinking about work and our day, then we'll be happy to tell you about our work and our day. When it comes to thinking about our work life, we just need it to be halftime when we get home—not overtime.

HOW CAN I GET HIM TO TALK MORE?

If I have to hear my husband say "Fine" one more time when I ask him how his day was, I think I'm going to flip. Can't he tell me a story or two about his day? I can't seem to get much out of him. He just comes home and wants to eat dinner without filling me in about what's going on at work. What can I do to get him to talk about his day?

"You know when my favorite time to talk about work is? While we're watching TV. The kids are in bed, we're both on the couch, and I know I have to squeeze my stories into two-minute commercial breaks," says Karl, 33. My feeling is that you can get even tough talkers to spout off like a runaway hose. First, don't ask him the ultimate mood-killing question: "How was your day?" A good interviewer asks specific questions

WHAT IT MEANS WHEN

. . . He drags his feet in terms of marriage
As the Magic 8-Ball says, "Outlook not so good." If he's stalling, there may be plenty of things that he loves about you and he doesn't want the relationship to end. But he suspects "signs pointing to yes" may be with someone else.

. . . He buys you an appliance for your birthday
When he buys something über-practical, he may not realize how unromantic you may view it—because he values gifts with use. In his mind, if you say you're always cold, presenting you with a space heater is the equivalent of two dozen long stems.

. . . He's still friends with his ex more than a year later
Take it as a positive that he's a good man, not as a negative that she's a threat. If their breakup didn't cause permanent damage, then chances are that, one, he's mature enough to let relationships evolve; two, he probably treated her well during their time together; and three, he didn't screw around on her. All good.

WONDERING WOMAN

He collects video games and baseball hats, yet claims not to understand why I buy so many pairs of shoes. Why can't he see the parallel?

Because video games and baseball hats cost less than twenty bucks, they never wear out, and we use them a hell of a lot more than just once or twice.

that elicit specific answers. So if you pepper him with "how was your day?" or "anything happen at work?" then the last thing he's going to do is launch into a 10-minute monologue about the saga of the disconnected server. Instead, wait until he's had time to get comfortable, crack a bottle, and veg. Then remember what he told you a few weeks ago about the boss, or his friend, or the new project he's working on. Specific questions lead to talking. General questions lead to grunting.

Male Mysteries

16

Percentage of men who list "housewife" as their spouse's ideal profession

WHY CAN'T HE FIND TIME TO TALK TO ME WHEN HE'S AT WORK?

One of my girlfriends has a husband who calls home from work two or three times a day to check in, make sure everything's okay, or just to talk about what's happening. My husband? He'll occasionally send me an e-mail or a text message about something to pick up at the store or something like that. And if I call him, which I try to do once a day, he's always distracted and rushes me off the phone. I don't expect him to interrupt what he's doing and talk to me for hours at a time. I just want him to call to check in with me every once in a while. Is it a lost cause to expect him to think about me during his work day and fill me in with what's going on?

Lots of times at work, a guy feels like he's in the zone—multitasking like a six-armed juggler. In his mind, he's obsessing about what he has to do, he's got 16 windows open on his laptop, and he has a meeting in 12 minutes. If you call him right then—in the middle of his sweet spot—then he's going to fall out of the zone, miss the shot, then derail. And if he's in that zone, he's—sorry to say—not thinking about when he should check in with you. "My girlfriend gets on me for not calling to say hi during the day. It's not like I'm opposed to it; it's just that I don't get that many breathers. It always seems that when she calls me, it's at the worst possible times," says Vincente, 32. How do you get him to check in with you? Stop checking in with him. One of the reasons why he isn't more active is because he knows—whether it's consciously or not—that you initiate the calls. It's really the same philosophy as dating: If you want him to chase, then back up.

WHAT CAN I DO TO GET HIM TO OPEN UP AND LOOSEN UP?

I know my boyfriend is really stressed at work. He's a lawyer who works 12- or 13-hour days. I can see how tired he is and I want to try to help him. But I know he keeps it all inside, and I'm afraid he's really going to run himself down if he just doesn't let it out every once in a while. Any suggestions?

You mean, besides a stiff martini and nightly backrubs? Okay then, how about a stiff martini and nightly backrubs? Fine, then. "I just went through the worst period of my work life—I had so many projects due that I just about freaked out. I pulled three all-nighters within about 10 days and I know I was a mess at home," says David, 33. "My wife was great about it. She knew I was having a tough stretch. She did all kinds of stuff without ever talking about my work, because she knew that talking about all I had to do would just make it worse. She went to her own job, then handled all the kid stuff, and even was up for a few stress-relieving sessions. When I had a day or two left, I finally told her that I felt like I was over the hump and started to relax more." When guys are ultra-stressed at work, they don't want to talk—they want to work. Or they want to think about work—and how they can take their level of stress down a few notches. Now, if they can reach a point when they can scale back on the working, then they'll be able to ramp up on the talking.

> **Male Mysteries**
>
> **17**
>
> Percentage of men who say that the amount they work is the thing that their wives or girlfriends complain about the most

MASCULINITY MASTERED: What You Now Know About Men

• If you ask us what happened at work when we get home, then nothing happened. If, instead, you ask us that question an hour or two later, plenty did.

• In the 12 hours we're at work, we feel like everyone's vying for a piece of us. When we get home, we want 20 minutes when nobody is.

• At home, we'd rather talk about the backstabbing, lies, deceit, and politics that happen on *Big Brother* than the kind that happens in our office.

SAY THIS TONIGHT!

The sexiest thing a woman ever said to Will, 30:

"I don't think we'll wake my parents, but let's try."

(on a visit to her family)

The sexiest thing Rena, 29, ever said to a man:

"I'm going to make your knees buckle."

(as she was pulling his trousers off)

Chapter 23

What Do Men Really Want in Bed?

How to find the perfect balance between predictable—and dangerous.

QUESTION: Gentlemen, what's something you would like to try in the bedroom with your wife or girlfriend? (Respondents could choose more than one.)

Toys:. . . . . 79 PERCENT

Watching porn: . . . . 78 PERCENT

Public sex: . . . . 77 PERCENT

Videotaping: . . . . 69 PERCENT

Light bondage:. . . . . 67 PERCENT

Role playing: . . . . 67 PERCENT

Grooming or shaving: . . . . 66 PERCENT

Threesomes:. . . . . 55 PERCENT

Swinging or swapping:. . . . . 24 PERCENT

OMETIMES, A MAN CAN TRACK HIS sexual future like The Weather Channel: He has a good idea when he's going to see sexual sunshine or have all businesses closed down because of the massive ice

storm. Sometimes, he has no idea what's coming: Maybe his play date will be spoiled by rain, or maybe he'll be showered with something he never saw coming.

Both aspects—the predictable and the unpredictable—serve their purposes. The predictable sex, in a way, de-stresses us—and comforts us—by letting us know that every sexual encounter won't have to take a double-overtime shift of pursuit and seduction in order to get there. (In a way, knowing we're going to get no sex does the same thing, because it means that we know we can get a good night's sleep.)

Curtis, a 33-year-old science teacher, says that he and wife have fallen into the routine of having sex almost every Friday night and every Sunday morning. "I guess for some people, they may not like the fact that sex looks like it's a scheduled appointment, but I don't look at it that way. When I wake up Friday, knowing that we're going to have sex that night, it's kind of like cerebral foreplay, even though we haven't even talked about it. It builds up, because I spend some of the day thinking about the fact that that's probably what we're going to do later on."

On the flip side, the unpredictable sex is what excites us—and it's one of the things that make us appreciate our relationship with you. With 21 percent of men saying the one thing they'd like to change about their sex life is "more experimentation" and "more variety," it's clear that men value spontaneity—an unexpected pair of panties on the doorknob. ("The best was a morning surprise. She woke me up and we just went at it from there," says Jay, 32. And Paul, 34, adds: "It was on our first anniversary. She walked in on me in the shower. I think the surprise is what made it the most memorable.")

Geoff, 37, a golf instructor, says the most memorable sex he's had with his wife occurred in the parking lot of a football

SAY THIS, NOT THAT!

SAY THIS: *Maybe we should try this flavored lube I bought today. I know just where to put it for a taste test.*

NOT: *Our sex life is so boring. We need to try something new.*

BECAUSE: *Don't just demand excitement, bring it on!*

SAY THIS: *Tonight I HAVE to sleep, but tomorrow night I'll rip your clothes off with my teeth.*

NOT: *I'm not in the mood.*

BECAUSE: *Rejection is always tough—even after years of marriage.*

SAY THIS: *Your penis is huge!*

NOT: *Silence.*

BECAUSE: *You love him.*

stadium before a game. "We were going to see a game, and we had the very back seat out of the van," he says. "We got to the game two hours before it started and she suggested we 'go back there.' I was shocked. She pulled down my trousers, performed oral sex on me, and then with me on my back, climbed on top of me. Unbelievable."

Perhaps Nathan, 33, a computer specialist, says it best. "Men don't necessarily want racier sex or wilder sex. I think men just want to be more attracted to their partners," he says. "Men don't get bored with their partners themselves, but maybe their looks. Just shake things up—get a new haircut, try new makeup, try to look just a little different and you'll find that your man will get a lot more interested. It's like the idea for 'enriching the environment' for animals in a zoo cage. Enrichment means doing novel things in the environment to keep the animals interested."

HOW DO I TURN HIM ON WITHOUT OVERDOING IT?

I've had sex with my new boyfriend a few times now, and I want to turn the volume up a little, but I don't want him to think I'm too experienced. When's a good time to bring in some, oh, value-added moves to the bedroom? And how can I do it without him thinking I'm a leather-and-cuffs queen?

The key here is to think of the difference between a scream and a whisper. While some of us are certainly into showy, turn-my-treadmill-into-a-sex-toy sex, many men pine for more subtle changes. Julie, 28, remembers the time her boyfriend was a groomsman. "Right before he walked down the aisle, I leaned over and told him that I wanted to go in the back for a quickie and that my 'little black dress' prohibited me from wearing underwear," she says. "He had to stand

WHAT IT MEANS WHEN

. . . One eye is on the TV while you're talking to him
He knows it's rude, but he thinks it'd be ruder to say, "Not now, dear, the last few minutes of this show trumps what you have to say, if you can just hang on to that thought for a few minutes."

. . . He says he doesn't want anything for his birthday
Anything electronics-, sports-, or music-related will be just fine.

. . . He says, "three or four," when you ask him how many drinks he had while he was out
Six or seven, as well as two shots.

WONDERING WOMAN

Dressing up. He looks so good and obviously feels good in a nice suit, so why doesn't he want to put one on more often?

For the same reason you don't like tights. We'll do it, but we'd rather be in sandals, cargo shorts, and the Atari T-shirt we found at a thrift store.

up at the wedding, but kept glancing in my direction. The entire reception he could barely keep his hands off me. It was hours of torture before I could make good on my seductive threat. And it made for an incredible night." It was the perfect storm of excitement and anticipation.

WHY DO MEN SOMETIMES THINK THEY HAVE A RIGHT TO SEX?

My husband and I were at a wedding and we both got pretty drunk—him a little more so than me. When we got back to the hotel room, he took off all his clothes and flopped down on the bed, like it was matter-of-fact that we were going to have sex. And that kinda pissed me off—that automatically because we're in a hotel room and at a wedding, he's going to get some. So nothing happened that night and I could tell he was disappointed. And then I got pissed—like he had a right to be upset that we didn't have sex. Why does he think he does?

On the surface, he knows that he should never expect sex. But, especially in his inebriated state, he was turning Pavlovian on you. Hotel? Check. Wedding? Check. Drunk and Horny? Check. With all systems in place, he concluded that there was only one conceivable outcome—two naked bodies getting busy together.

"One night, my girlfriend and I finished off two bottles of wine," says Tom, 30, a pharmacist. "And she was just much more uninhibited. She talked dirty, she moved more, she was into it. It was good because it was no holds barred, anything goes, nobody taps out. We were both completely into doing whatever needed to be done to give the other amazing sex." It makes sense, especially when alcohol's involved, to give a guy a heads up that there'll be no, um, heads down that night.

HE SAID . . .

How satisfied he is with his partner's sexual performance

Extremely satisfied:	**16 percent**
Very satisfied:	**26 percent**
Satisfied:	**26 percent**
Somewhat satisfied:	**23 percent**
Not at all satisfied:	**9 percent**

WHAT DO GUYS REALLY YEARN FOR IN BED?

If you had to rank what men really want in bed, give me the bottom line. What really satisfies a man?

It depends entirely on the man. Some men are into anonymous sex. ("My best was when I met a woman who gave me oral sex as the sun came up while I was lying naked on the beach," says Rich, 26.) Some men are more interested in deep sex. ("The best sex I had was when my girlfriend and I didn't need to talk at all. We just connected so completely that everything flowed naturally," says Andrew, 38.) But the best sex of all is a combination of wild physical abandon and deep emotional connection. Sixty-two percent of men say their sexual experience is best when they're connected both emotionally and physically. William, a 32-year-old building contractor, says it best: "The best sex I had was an all-night romp, which was one-half animalistic and one-half emotional."

Male Mysteries

61

Percentage of men who don't think their partners are sexually adventurous enough

MASCULINITY MASTERED: What You Now Know About Men

- Don't dismiss a sexual routine as being boring—at least not to him.

- Few things will ever top you throwing him a sexual surprise party.

- We need both physical *and* emotional passion to feel sated.

WHAT'S THE ONE THING HE'LL NEVER TELL HIS WIFE OR GIRLFRIEND ABOUT WHAT SHE'S LIKE IN BED?

- "She needs to give more than she receives."
- "She needs to initiate every once in a while."
- "She holds back too much, "
- "She could be more active. Take me, baby!"
- "She's unadventurous because she feels if you do something you've done with someone else, you must be thinking of that other person."
- "I would never tell her that she didn't turn me on as much as a previous girlfriend, not if I want to keep my testicles anyway."
- "Be more confident in your looks."
- "When she's on top, she's very robotic."
- "Make more noise."
- "I enjoy doing different things, but I don't want her to think I'm odd."
- "She doesn't grind as much as I'd like."

SAY THIS TONIGHT!

The sexiest thing a woman ever said to Noah, 23:

"I want to ride you into the sunset."

The sexiest thing Natalie, 29, ever said to a man:

"Pull over. I need you to make love to me right now."

Chapter 24

What Inspires a Man to Marry?

How to tap into his inner romantic and build his forever-together fantasy.

QUESTION: Single guys, do you see yourself marrying the woman you're dating now?

Yes:. . . . . 41 PERCENT

No:. . . . . 14 PERCENT

Not sure: . . . . 45 PERCENT

YOU MAY THINK THAT MEN HAVE ABOUT as much use for marriage as a bald man has for hair mousse. Or that if men picked the wedding march, it would be "Another One Bites the Dust." Or that we view lifelong commitment sort of like that horror movie, *The Ring*: First you see the ring, then you die.

Well, here's a secret: Guys love the idea of marriage.

No, maybe we don't care if the cake has two tiers or three or if the invitation paper is almond or vanilla or if the bridesmaids wear their hair up or down (okay, we do prefer down). Maybe we don't buy bridal magazines or check train lengths or debate the politics of choosing one cousin over another for the sacred position of flower girl.

But you know what? We love weddings—and not just when they present *Wedding Crashers*–style opportunities. In fact, the wedding's even better when it's ours.

▶ *"Best day in my life: When my kids were born. Second best day: My wedding. I had a blast (and I didn't even drink a lot). It was just amazing to have most of my friends and family all in one place,"* says Brian, 28.

▶ *"There are very few times when you get to be the center of attention like you are at your wedding. Yeah, I got sick of answering the same questions about the honeymoon, but without sounding too much like a girl, it was pretty cool to feel like the whole room was smiling at you,"* says Blake, 34.

▶ *"I remember my friend, as we were planning it, saying that a wedding is just one big performance—where everybody takes their place, does their job, is on stage for the whole audience to see,"* says Todd, 27. *"She was right. It was like this one big concert, and you were on a high the whole time because everybody was so into it."*

▶ *"Our band rocked, and I've never danced so much in my life,"* says Ed, 32. *"This is going to sound weird to say because I obviously love my wife, but it was like the whole night was license for beautiful women to come up and dance with you. It wasn't anything sexual or anything like that, but, damn."*

But just as with sex, you can be more attuned to the foreplay of a marriage, while we're more deeply focused on the main event. And that's one reason why the planning period has so many conflicts. "My fiancée and I had a pretty big fight about our wedding," says Kel, 30, a physiotherapist. "Her family was pushing for a really formal and traditional reception, and my

---

SAY THIS, NOT THAT!

SAY THIS: *You make me so happy!*

NOT: *All of my friends are getting engaged.*

BECAUSE: *The fact that everyone else is doing it is a very bad reason to get married.*

SAY THIS: *I love you. I want to have YOUR baby.*

NOT: *I want to have a baby.*

BECAUSE: *He wants to feel like this is about you and him, not you and a baby.*

family was pushing for a more casual one. I think they may have even mentioned the word *luau*, which really threw my fiancée for a loop. It was starting to escalate, and I could go either way on it, but I just decided that nothing about the wedding planning was worth spoiling the day over. I told my family that in conflicts, what the bride wants beats everything."

That's probably where some of the confusion lies. Because we acquiesce to virtually all wedding decisions, it doesn't mean we think of our wedding as just another Saturday night.

WHY DOESN'T HE CARE MORE ABOUT THE WEDDING?

I remember when one of my friends got married. Her husband-to-be was involved in everything. He helped pick flowers, the cake, everything. It was like he was really excited about getting married. My fiancé is the exact opposite. It doesn't matter what question I ask, his answers are either "I don't care" or "whatever you want." All I want is for him to have an opinion, to act a little interested in what our wedding will be like. It's going to be one of the biggest days of our lives and he acts like we're planning a trip to the supermarket. Does he really have no interest in these details?

He may not register an opinion about fonts and flowers, but don't mistake his indifference over things as an indifference to you or the wedding. "When I got engaged, I backed off. I had the philosophy that this wasn't my day; this was hers. And if raspberry icing was what made her happy than who the hell was I to stand in the way of raspberry icing?" says Daunte, 32. "I think she wanted me to go to more appointments and all that preparation stuff, but I just viewed it like she was a truck and I was deer—I got the hell out of her way so I didn't get hit." But here's the conflict: A man doesn't want to be treated like perfect-couple ornamentation—just sitting at appointments and with planners and with vendors without making any contributions at all. Don't ask him to be there just to be there. If he's going to spend the time listening to all of the options, then you have to be open to hear what he's saying, even if you have a different opinion.

Male Mysteries

82

Percentage of men who think they'll stay with their wives till death do them part *(MH)*

WHAT IT MEANS WHEN

. . . He says, "any," when you ask him his favorite sex position

Start kissing while standing up, then, after some groping and more kissing, take each other's clothes off, move down to the bed and alternate giving oral sex to each other. He then slides on top of you, and then you switch positions several times (missionary, then doggie), finally ending up with you on top of him so he can see all of your body, touch you all over, and have your hands and lips go crazy all over him. Not that he's thought all that much about it.

. . . He pulls you on top of him

He's spent his whole life controlling the joystick—how fast it goes and how far into the game he can get. There's something especially exciting about relinquishing the control and letting you man the controls, push the buttons, and take the game in any darn direction you want.

. . . He says, "no," when you ask him if porn turns him on

His small in-emergencies-only stash is on the top shelf of his closet, in the back left corner, in a box.

HOW WORRIED SHOULD I BE ABOUT THE STAG PARTY?

I know my fiancé's best friend, and I know what kind of guy he is. And I just know that the stag party is going to be pretty out of control. I'm not worried that my fiancé's going to do anything. Well, I guess maybe I am. I just don't like the idea of him drinking lots of tequila while he's surrounded by lots and lots of near-naked women. How worried should I be? And what do guys really get out of the whole last hurrah?

You should be worried—if you're marrying his crazy best friend. But if you're confident about the guy you're marrying, be confident about how he'll conduct himself at the party. Look, a stag party isn't all about the Ts, the As, and the G-strings (though he likely won't complain about any of them). It's not about purposely worrying you or making you jealous. And it's not about the tequila shots or the belly button shots either. It's about him being the star of his own party for a few hours, that's all. You know all the attention you get and the bonding you have during the 12 months or 24 months or however long your engagement lasts? He gets the same thing out of his stag party—only it's measured in a few hours instead of a few months (or years).

SHOULD I GO RING SHOPPING WITH HIM?

Some of my girlfriends have gone ring shopping with their boyfriends. I just find it terribly unromantic, but I also don't want him to get a ring that isn't "me." I'm not sure if he wants help picking it out or if he wants to be left alone (assuming, of course, we are going to be going down this road). What's the best way to help him

pick the right ring without spoiling what should be one of the most memorable, romantic moments of my life?

This is the time-honored way by which brides gently manipulate their intendeds: Tell your best friend what you want and have her find a way to subtly bring it up with him. Guys don't necessarily want to be the decision makers when it comes to choosing the engagement ring; what they want is the *illusion* that they're the decision makers. Openly dictating something like this ruins that illusion; cleverly manipulating it from behind the scenes, however, provides a welcome guidebook. "My girlfriend showed me exactly what kind of ring she wanted, and that took the pressure off me, because Lord knows I didn't want to mess up that decision, but looking back, I really wish she didn't know it was coming," says Jackson, 38.

Your fiancé gets one shot to construct the story that you'll tell friends, family, kids, everybody. Give him some room to make it come out right—for both of you.

MASCULINITY MASTERED: What You Now Know About Men

• If you'd like us to be involved and active in the wedding planning, then don't have a preordained script for the way everything is going to be before we even start talking about it. If you want us involved, you need to let us express an opinion.

• Men want to make as few decisions as possible. Just go with the flow on that, okay?

• We only want—and expect—this to happen once. So let's do it right. (Then let's have the same philosophy on the honeymoon.)

WONDERING WOMAN

I'm not against porn, but I am bothered when he's sneaky about it. Why not just include me in the fun?

Three reasons: He finds it incredibly impolite to be looking at other naked women while you're kissing his chest. He doesn't think you'll be the slightest bit turned on by women with a triple-E cup size screaming like hyenas. And there's a sexual-fantasy slice of his brain that he'd like to keep to himself.

SAY THIS TONIGHT!

The sexiest thing a woman ever said to Randy, 35:

"Ich will mit du schlafen."

("I want to sleep with you," in German.)

The sexiest thing Diana, 26, ever said to a man:

"That shirt would look great on my floor."

Chapter 25

What Do Men Really Want in Love?

The truth about what keeps men in love for decades—and the simple formula you need for ensuring long-term happiness.

QUESTION: Men, how often would you like to have sex?

Couple of times a month or less: . . . . 6 PERCENT

Once a week: . . . . 8 PERCENT

Twice a week: . . . . 22 PERCENT

Three times a week: . . . . 28 PERCENT

More than three times a week: . . . . 38 PERCENT

How often are you currently having sex?

Couple of times a month or less: . . . . 58 PERCENT

Once a week: . . . . 15 PERCENT

Twice a week: . . . . 12 PERCENT

Three times a week: . . . . 6 PERCENT

More than three times a week: . . . . 9 PERCENT

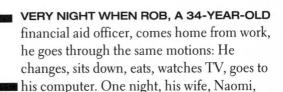

VERY NIGHT WHEN ROB, A 34-YEAR-OLD financial aid officer, comes home from work, he goes through the same motions: He changes, sits down, eats, watches TV, goes to his computer. One night, his wife, Naomi, wanted to mix things up. "We were watching TV," Naomi says, "and I got up to go to the bathroom and came back to the sofa naked. I obviously looked sexy because we didn't watch TV. I mean, we didn't watch TV for the rest of the night."

Rob got what every man wants in his long-term relationship: A curveball. The fact that it was a sexual curveball just meant that this pitch had extra mustard on it.

Just as we want our bedroom activity to have the appropriate ratio of predictability and surprise, we want the same for our lives in the rest of the house, too. The kitchen. The living room. The bathroom. (Okay, maybe not the bathroom.) We want the stability of a woman who's strong, who's predictable, who's a good mother, who's passionate about what she loves, who's smart, who's a stable influence for us—and for our future kids. "Everybody says that the biggest downer in a relationship is doing the same thing over and over," says Bryan, 30, who's been married for six years. "You want to hear about our ruts? Friday nights, we watch movies with pizza and wine. Saturday, we usually go for a long trail ride or hike for half a day, then eat a late lunch at the local diner. Sunday mornings, we sleep in, if you want to call it sleeping. Call it a routine if you want, but I think it's working out okay."

Male Mysteries

80

Percentage of men who believe love doesn't have a shelf life

Why is routine so crucial? Because a woman without predictability is also a woman free of responsibility—and that's not the kind of woman we want to be committed to. We want to be committed to the woman who pays bills on time, who's committed to her career and/or to her family, who's stable enough to stabilize us. Add in a dash of free-spiritedness and an ability to make (well-thought-out) whimsical decisions, and we've found the woman who understands the yin and yang of what it means to satisfy a man. Completely.

SAY THIS, NOT THAT!

SAY THIS: *You're 45 and you want to start a rock band, how cool!*

NOT: *You're 45 and you want to start a rock band, how lame!*

BECAUSE: *Rock bands are fun—and life should be fun, no matter how old you are.*

HOW DO I KNOW WHAT'S TOO ADVENTUROUS FOR HIM?

We've been seeing each other for well over a year and I always like trying to keep things spicy. One night I got undressed at my office, put on my coat, wore it on the bus, and showed up at his place with a smile and a surprise. But later, my boyfriend took more of a lecturing tone with me, telling me that it was dangerous, that I really shouldn't have done that, on and on, almost like he was my parent. Am I wrong in being angry that he didn't appreciate me doing all of this essentially for him?

Certainly, men love their share of risk-taking. ("We managed to do it in a lagoon in Jamaica, in broad daylight, in front of hundreds of people, without getting caught," says Brendan, 23.) But as a relationship progresses, there's such a thing as good risk and bad risk. In his mind, he's thinking, *What if you got caught on the way? What if some slimeball tried to feel you up? What if the wind blew your coat open?* Oh, you don't have to worry too much: He appreciated the dividend he received for your risk, but I think his reaction was a good one. It showed that he's as interested in protecting you from danger (and embarrassment) as he is in enjoying you.

HOW DO I PREVENT RELATIONSHIP RUTS?

I've been in two pretty long-term relationships. One was about a year, and one lasted three years. Every relationship reaches a point where it gets into that routine, or rut, or whatever you want to call it. I'm curious about what men think about those routines and what they think women should do. I'm now eight months into a new relationship and I just don't want this guy to ever feel bored with me or with our routine.

WHAT IT MEANS WHEN

. . . He won't give you his password

It may be your test of trust. But even if he's not instant messaging his ex, he'll do what he can to keep his password private because to him, it's symbolic of his personal space. Push him for it, and he's going to feel choked. And he'll eventually find a way to slip your hold.

. . . He says he can't live without you

He's listened to too much Queen.

. . . He lashes out at you after you break up with him

He'll be calling you in a couple weeks, pleading for your forgiveness, after many hours of listening to Queen.

WONDERING WOMAN

Why do guys have to have a movie quote for every situation?

You talking to me? He's not sure you can handle the truth, so it seems like what we've got here is a failure to communicate. Frankly, my dear, he doesn't give a damn that you don't like that he quotes movies. Why? Because using movie lines means he can convey any emotion at any time without ever having to do it himself. Hoo-ah!

Passage excerpted from: *The Godfather, A Few Good Men, Cool Hand Luke, Gone with the Wind,* and *Scent of a Woman*

A routine is something you do wearing your dance class outfit. A rut is something we do after you take it off. Seriously, though, there's such a thing as a good routine (morning sex is a routine, but no one's complaining). Where it changes into a rut is when the routine starts to leave you feeling empty. "Sometimes my girlfriend acts really interested and excited, and teases the whole night, and then she turns into her usual 'pillow flower' when she gets naked, and it's getting old," says Pat, 32. The only way you can ensure that your relationship doesn't get stuck in a rut is to make sure there's always a little part of him that never knows when you'll initiate the next romp, the next living room streak show, or the next random butt squeeze. Keep us on our toes and we'll always hope to keep you in the picture.

MASCULINITY MASTERED: What You Now Know About Men

• Routine isn't what's bad about relationships. Boring routines are what's bad about relationships.

• One unexpected naked strut: Priceless.

• As a relationship grows, the right mix is three parts stability to one part free spirit. Stability provides the base we'll need to live our day-to-day life, while the free spirit is what makes it fun to live.

SAY THIS TONIGHT!

The sexiest thing a woman ever said to Drew, 26:
"You won't forget tonight."

The sexiest thing Julia, 33, ever said to a man:
"I could devour you like a piece of chocolate cake, lick you up one side and down the other."

Index